INVESTIGATING THE ALMOST
PERFECT MURDERS

'The primary object of an efficient police is the prevention of crime: the next that of detection and punishment of offenders if crime is committed. To these ends all the efforts of police must be directed. The protection of life and property, the preservation of public tranquillity, and the absence of crime, will alone prove whether those efforts have been successful and whether the objects for which the police were appointed have been attained.'

Sir Richard Mayne 1829

INVESTIGATING
THE ALMOST PERFECT
MURDERS

THE CASE OF RUSSELL CAUSLEY
AND OTHER CRIMES

ANTHONY NOTT, MBE

PEN & SWORD
TRUE CRIME

First published in Great Britain in 2020 by
Pen & Sword True Crime
An imprint of
Pen & Sword Books Ltd
Yorkshire – Philadelphia

ISBN 978 1 52676 338 9

Printed and bound in England
By TJ International Ltd.

Pen & Sword Books Ltd incorporates the Imprints
of Pen & Sword Books Archaeology, Atlas, Aviation,
Battleground, Discovery, Family History, History,
Maritime, Military, Naval, Politics, Railways, Select,
Transport, True Crime, Fiction, Frontline Books,
Leo Cooper, Praetorian Press, Seaforth Publishing,
Wharncliffe and White Owl.

For a complete list of Pen & Sword titles please contact

PEN & SWORD BOOKS LIMITED
47 Church Street, Barnsley, South Yorkshire, S70 2AS,
England
E-mail: enquiries@pen-and-sword.co.uk
Website: www.pen-and-sword.co.uk

or

PEN AND SWORD BOOKS
1950 Lawrence Rd, Havertown, PA 19083, USA
E-mail: uspen-and-sword@casematepublishers.com
Website: www.penandswordbooks.com

Contents

Acknowledgements

I would like to thank Mrs Ursula Jeffries for reading the first draft of this book and reminding me of the inequality and difficulties endured by many women and minority groups during the 1970s; a time which saw great change. I would also like to thank Malcolm Davey and his wife Jan (who is also the Editor of the Free Portland News) for their proof reading of these recollections and devoting acres of time to the checking and re-checking of these accounts.

The presentation of this book in its current form would not have been possible without the professional guidance, encouragement and punctilious adherence to English grammar by Carol Trow, herself an accomplished author.

Whilst these recollections are largely mine, I am grateful to the many former officers of the Dorset Police who have either assisted me with their memory of events; or checked what I have written to ensure the accuracy of these accounts. Most officers I worked with have allowed me to use their real names, but in several instances, I have substituted pseudonyms where those concerned would prefer to remain anonymous. It is a luxury, rarely enjoyed by crime writers and criminologists, to have access to so many experienced detectives closest to the events and their confidence in me to disclose what they have.

I would like to give my special thanks to Samantha Gillingham and her son Neil for their help and cooperation in my recounting of the investigation into the murder of her mother, by her father Russell Causley. Without Samantha's drive and determination, he may have got away with this killing and achieved the perfect murder. He did not.

I should also like to thank my wife Judith profusely who had to live through these cases, putting up with my worries, doubts and frustration, plus my boring her into submission when I recounted mind-numbing detailed facts about the ins and outs of matters which occurred in a world she does not understand.

Anthony Nott
Dorset
Spring 2019

Preface

I originally wrote recollections of my police service, both in the UK, the Balkans and Middle East between 2010 and 2015. I was fortunate to find a publisher, but what I had written exceeded their desired word count and was deemed too different, in that one part concerned policing in the UK and the other more hostile environments abroad. Consequently, I split the book into two distinct parts; the second half was published in 2017 by Pen and Sword Books Ltd under the title *Investigating Organised Crime and War Crimes*. My transition from mainstream civilian policing to international policing came at a critical juncture for me, when I was caught up in the maelstrom of a suspected miscarriage of justice case arising from a murder trial and as a consequence, suspicion falling on me of perverting the course of justice in that case. This matter was referred to in passing in *Investigating Organised Crime and War Crimes* but is referred to in more detail in this book as the case itself, that of Russell Causley, is dealt with in depth. I apologise for having to repeat in the last chapter of this book, some of the same events from the first chapter of my earlier published work, as the transition from one segment of my life to another is relevant to both accounts.

Having worked to proof read and perfect – in the broadest sense of the word – *Investigating Organised Crime and War Crimes* I set to work to complete an account of my earlier service which is now set out here. I have added two separate chapters and a further case study of the complicated investigation into the murder of a homosexual man, when society's attitudes were different from what they are today. This book starts in 1971, when I joined the Metropolitan Police, in what was then a very different world. Irish Republican-motivated terrorism was just making an impression on the UK mainland; the rise of fundamentalist Islamic terrorism was unheard of –

at least in the UK – and the police were broadly trusted to investigate major crime with propriety. All this would change with a multitude of miscarriage of justice cases being heaped up one upon another, a plethora of corruption scandals involving very senior police officers linked to organised crime families and finally being labelled as institutionally racist in the Macpherson Report. Police evidence was to be viewed with great suspicion and public confidence dropped to an all-time low. New legislation with more rigorous and reliable procedures – such as tape-recorded interviews – were introduced in due course and after a massive culture change the police service eventually recovered the respect they had lost from the public whom they serve.

The investigation of major crime is very much a team effort involving all of the various departments in the police. But, outside of that is the very important role played by the lawyers of the Crown Prosecution Service and then the prosecuting barristers, all of whom are essential to the successful conviction of offenders. The most important player in all this panoply of crime investigation is usually the general public, where quite often people from humble backgrounds arise to come forward and testify in the forbidding arena of the court room and deliver damning evidence, notwithstanding feelings of trepidation, fear and humiliation, and all for little or no personal reward.

I am able to recount details of cases I was investigating because I was either there and have referred to court files of the case in question, or I have had the luxury of interviewing a considerable number of police officers who were involved in every stage of the cases cited.

I have deliberately avoided disclosing police operational tactics where these means are largely unknown and their revelation would help those I have spent most of my life pursuing. This does not detract from the flavour of the book which I hope captures the dedication, flaws and sometimes self-doubt, of those charged with investigating the crimes described.

I have tried to capture the atmosphere and ethos, problems and successes of the police during the last decades of the twentieth century into the present. This was a time of rapid change, but one which maintained a focus around policing, with and for the community. After the financial crisis of 2008, UK police budgets were slashed over five years by twenty percent which saw police stations close, the police retreat from the high street and eventually sharp rises in crime. I have described a period when the police and in particular local detectives knew their community, particularly the bad eggs in it and were, I like to think, ahead of the game. This book sets out how that close relationship between police and public is so vital in detecting crime and thereby leading to its prevention in the first place. There is a misunderstanding amongst our intelligentsia that policing is now in a different world, everything is internet based and that crime and disorder have somehow moved into another virtual reality. That is true in part, but people are people, human nature has changed little since as a species we started to crawl over the planet; 'face time', as it is now called, is still paramount, in my view, in human relations.

That a few people are evil is a concept not accepted by some members of our society. Evil acts are frequently ascribed to be the work of the mentally ill who need treatment; those who have been radicalised, who would otherwise not have embarked on careers of torture and murder; or the fault of social media which some-how indoctrinated otherwise healthy individuals. Having been face-to-face with the perpetrators of crime for almost forty decades, I have come across evil people very infrequently. Those I have dealt with exhibit characteristics of being sane, intelligent, personable and cunning. Murder to them is a means to an end, or the end in itself when visual images no longer give them the excitement they crave. These people, I have found, possess an inborn arrogance, a feeling of superiority over their fellow mortals and they are almost always complete narcissists. Despite the scientific age in which we live, I believe that evil is abroad in the world, as will be seen in the following pages.

The Red Squirrel

A lawyer advertised for a clerk. The next morning his office was crowded with applicants – all bright, many suitable. He asked them wait until they had all arrived and then ranged them in a semi-circle and said he would tell them a story, note their comments and judge from that whom he would choose.

'A certain farmer,' began the lawyer, 'was troubled with a red squirrel that got in through a hole in his barn and stole his corn seed. He resolved to kill the squirrel at the first opportunity. Seeing him go into the hole one night, he took his old flintlock blunderbuss and fired off a great spread of lead balls. Sparks flew from the old gun and caught some hay on fire which quickly spread to the barn.'

'Did the barn burn down?' asked one of the boys.

The lawyer without answering continued, 'And seeing the barn on fire, the farmer seized a pail of water and ran to put it out.'

'Did he put it out?' another wanted to know.

'As he passed inside, the door shut and the barn was soon in flames, which is when the hired girl ran in with more water from the pump.'

'Was she trapped inside?' one asked.

'Could they form a chain from the water pump to the barn?' wondered another boy.

The lawyer went on without answering. 'Then the old lady came out and all was noise and confusion and everybody was trying to put out the fire.'

'Did any-one burn up?' asked another.

'Then the fire engine arrived but the hose pipe had a hole in it.'

'Could they use rags to wrap around the hole?' a boy excitedly suggested.

The lawyer said, 'There, that will do; you have all shown great interest in the story,' but observing one bright eyed fellow in deep silence, he said 'Now, my little man, what have you to say?'

The little fellow blushed, grew uneasy and stammered out, 'I want to know what became of that squirrel; that's what I want to know.'

'You'll do,' said the lawyer; 'You are my man; you have not been distracted by a confusion of barn burning and hired girls and water pails. *You have kept your eye on the squirrel.*'

Lancashire Constabulary Advanced CID training course 1983. Successful students are awarded a red squirrel tie.

CHAPTER 1

A Constable is Born

I was born several years after the end of the Second World War, in a generation which became known as 'the baby boomers.' I clearly remember my early years growing up in south Devon, years which saw real austerity and food rationing, which only came to an end in 1954. My mother and father were outstanding parents bringing up my sister and me with much love and devotion. My dad was a local authority planning officer and my mum was a cockney girl who had grown up in the Isle of Dogs in London's docklands and worked in a shoe shop. They had both lived through the Blitz and spent many an evening in Marble Arch tube station playing monopoly with their friends whilst London was being bombed above them. They were a tough generation and their parents even tougher; my grandfather had died of his wounds after months of living in lice ridden trenches under constant bombardment, in the First World War. My generation would never have to endure these horrors. Many of my school friends were Polish whose parents had fled the Nazis, some of whom had flown for the RAF in the Battle of Britain. Apart from their rather funny names, such as Janowski and Ladislaw, there was no difference between us. We all played rugby and were mildly irritating with the girls.

I was more interested in sport than academic study and made the usual wrong assumptions of youth, that everything would be handed to me on a plate, without me having to do much more than just turn up at school each day. I flunked my GCE O-levels because I mucked around, instead of working hard and I had to retake them. I ended up with four, and that was after a great effort. I had always wanted to be a policeman having been an eager fan of the popular television series *Dixon of Dock Green*. I still harboured the fat-headed idea that as soon as I applied to join the police, I would be welcomed with open arms.

My great grandfather was Sergeant Abraham Nott of the Devon Constabulary, who had arrested John (Babbacombe) Lee for murder in 1884. He had originally been called to a house in Babbacombe near Torquay, Devon, belonging to a Miss Emma Keyse. He found her body in the lounge which had been wrapped in a carpet and set on fire; she had been killed with an axe. He carried out a meticulous search at the murder scene, even by today's standards and questioned the servants including one, a former sailor, called John Lee. My great grandfather noticed blood on his trousers and arrested him after finding more blood in his bedroom. Lee was subsequently found guilty at the quarter sessions and sentenced to death. However, things did not go according to plan and as a result of witchcraft, some said, or more likely the rain swelling the wood of the scaffold on the night before his execution, caused the trapdoor to jam as he stood on it with a rope around his neck. His death sentence was commuted to imprisonment for life and the servant Lee, became famous as 'the man they couldn't hang.' Fairport Convention recorded an album about Babbacombe Lee in the 1970s. Perhaps he was the man who they shouldn't have tried to hang.

I felt policing was in my blood and when I was sixteen, I applied to join the Metropolitan Police cadets. I thought that London was where all the action was and I quite liked all the well-dressed girls, as they appeared far more sensual than their country sisters. So it was London then. Well no actually; I got turned down. Apparently, my eyesight was not up to the very high standard demanded of police cadets and I came down to earth with a bump. So I took up another career, that of being a tax collector. I thought it seemed kind of cool to work in an office with the label of civil servant. I imagined I was a Whitehall mandarin, but my heart was in the police.

When I was nineteen, I tried once more to join the police, this time the local force. I was turned down again, on this occasion by the uniform sergeant who came to my house to conduct a preliminary interview. I didn't even get past the first stage; I guess he thought if I wasn't good enough for the Met, I wouldn't be good enough for the Devon and Cornwall Constabulary. I didn't want to admit the unthinkable, that maybe I *wasn't* good enough. Nonetheless, I wasn't done yet. I knew that the Met at the time were undermanned and had recently allowed constables to wear spectacles with the aim of recruiting more officers. At the same time, by sheer coincidence and good fortune, a recruiting team from the Met were in Torquay looking for country boys and girls to join up. I impressed the recruiters and somehow stumbled through the selection process to end up being accepted. The Goddess Fortuna appeared to choose to be my travelling companion through life, as good luck was to come my way more often than not.

I was just twenty-one years old in 1971, as green as grass, dressed in a sober manner in sports jacket, shirt and tie and good practical shoes. I could not understand the radical politics of the time and thought that the war in Vietnam was being fought in my interest to stop the communists invading the world through the domino effect. I didn't much care for the hippy and LSD culture of the time and was more into Beethoven than the Beatles. I was about as square a peg as you could get into a round hole and my ability to get on with girls was correspondingly disastrous. This was the year that US forces in Vietnam assisted the South Vietnamese army to invade Laos. Captain William Calley of the US army was convicted of killing twenty-two Vietnamese civilians in the My Lai massacre and Simon and Garfunkel sang 'Bridge over Troubled Water' – how right they were.

The Metropolitan Police Training School at Hendon came as a bit of a shock. No sooner had all the recruits on my intake assembled, when we were told that about twenty percent of us wouldn't make it. That happened to be about right. There was none of the fluffy sitting around in a circle on bean bags and developing our minds kind of approach. No, it was all about parrot fashion learning and there was a lot of it. Our first evening's homework was to be able to recite the next day 'The Primary Objects of an Efficient Police' by Sir Richard Maine, the first commissioner of the Met, in 1829 – see the beginning of this book. Whilst this may seem to many a very old-fashioned approach, it in fact instilled in me the credo of the police and what I was to be about. Once you know the doctrine, you know exactly what is expected of you. I learnt Acts of Parliament, definitions of legal terms and a multitude of police procedures this way. A police officer on the beat must know his or her powers of entry into property, search and arrest with precision. Instant decision- making is necessary and you don't usually have half an hour to consult a law book. Having passed out of Hendon Training School I was posted to Holborn police station in Central London. I was as proud as punch at being a policeman and couldn't wait to get to work.

My head swelled sufficiently in the early days, so much so that I perfected a technique of walking along my beat whilst getting an unobtrusive look at myself in shop windows, and I liked what I saw. It all turned to sand one day when I was walking through the street market in Leather Lane just off Hatton Garden, when I was fully engrossed in watching my reflection. Unfortunately, I didn't notice the support for the shop's blind awning above my head and it knocked my helmet clean off. It caused great merriment amongst the cockney stall holders and my utter humiliation. I sneaked off round a side alley and found an alternative route back to the police station. Walking the beat is in fact a real craft, putting aside low shop awnings.

We were given a set beat for a month which covered the three shifts of six to two early turn; two to ten late turn; and ten to six night shift. During that month the beat bobby would become familiar with all the sounds, people and patterns of his particular area. I knew that between 7 pm to 11 pm cars may be broken into or stolen from New Compton Street near Soho and surrounding area, where people parked to go into the West End, so that was a good place for a policeman to loiter. I knew that heroin was bought, sold and used in and around Shaftsbury Avenue near Gerrard Street and burglaries occurred during the night in and around the diamond centre of Hatton Garden. I observed with awe how senior constables talked to people from the slightly insane to the rough East End or south London villain. The older senior constables were looked up to for their experience and skill. It was from the likes of these officers that I learned how to question suspects, communicate with the man and woman in the street, and interrogate witnesses to gently extract their best recollections of an event in full. The start of duty each day took the form of a briefing called a 'parade' when constables would be assigned their beat by the sergeant. He would also read out reports detailing local crimes, suspects who were currently wanted on warrant, and patterns of crime such as from where and when burglaries and thefts were taking place and so on. Towards the end of the 'parade' the inspector would march into the room and the officers would all stand to attention and produce their pocket book, whistle and truncheon. He would then walk down the line of officers in a very authoritarian manner and comment on any one not smartly attired. After this ceremony was completed the briefing would continue. Inspectors were routinely saluted in those days, but I am afraid all this discipline has since disappeared and the force is the poorer for it.

London was an exciting place to be in the early 1970s. The hippy culture had become a pandemic, Carnaby Street was hip and London really did swing. There was also alleged to be free love everywhere, but everywhere I was, it seemed to be some other place. Too much Beethoven, I guess! The Metropolitan Police really was on another planet in those days. Whilst the vast majority of police officers were hard working and frequently assaulted and occasionally killed on duty, the spectre of corruption appeared all too often over the force. The Commander of the 'Flying Squad', Ken Drury, was arrested for corruption, which had occurred as a result of his unhealthy association with Jim Humphries; a club owner and pornographer, and his wife Rusty, a well-known stripper. CID officers from the 'Obscene Publications Squad' were caught recycling seized pornographic material. Hauls of drugs were turning up showing traces of aluminium powder, which was of a type used by crime scene examiners to highlight fingerprints. So, it wasn't quite like *Dixon of Dock Green*. However, that wasn't all. Because of the lack of forensic capability and the strict adherence by professional criminals to remain silent under questioning, apart from 'I want my brief,' a culture was in existence of trying to get the job done by other means. This was engaged in by officers who believed the suspect was guilty but did not have the evidence to convict him, so took it upon themselves to be judge and jury as well. This was later called 'noble cause corruption,' but in its day referred to as a 'verbal' or inventing a reply from the accused. This culture was deeply embedded in the Met at that time and I suspect had grown up over many years. It was shortly to be inevitably revealed in miscarriage of justice trial after miscarriage of justice trial. The high-water mark was the acquittal of the 'Birmingham Six', the six suspected IRA bombers who were believed to have killed twenty people in Central Birmingham. Their convictions were quashed on appeal in 1991, after it had come to light that they had been threatened and beaten while in custody in order to extract confessions. After this, a seismic shift took place within the whole service, the level of professionalism increased and a zero tolerance of malpractice developed.

Despite the above, and while county forces were far less susceptible to these problems, I learnt my trade of speaking to people from all walks of life. I got used to dealing with some sad and broken members of society, many of them alcoholics, drug addicts, victims of abuse and the much neglected mentally ill. This ability to engage with the multi-faceted, multi-layered and polyglot society that is Britain is one of the most important skills a police officer must have, not least when exercising the power to stop and search members of the public.

This most important tool has been in legislation since the Metropolitan Police was founded in 1829 and the wording giving the police this power was learnt parrot fashion by all recruits. It enables police officers to stop and search people and vehicles where the officer suspects stolen goods or weapons may be found. I used this power regularly to engage, not alienate the local people, who lived on my beat. The trick was to convince them that it was in their interest to allow me to search them for knives as I did not want them getting killed. So, I learnt from older policemen how to talk to the local youngsters, warn them about carrying weapons and give them the opportunity to hand over any knives they may have been in possession of, with the promise I would not arrest them. The usual claim was that they were only carrying a knife for their own protection; this is not a defence in law and I made sure to deliver a lecture on the point. I managed to recover a fair number of weapons in this voluntary manner and got to know the local youngsters much better. It may seem odd that a police officer can give this kind of local amnesty, but this discretion given to constables is an important power in policing by consent, preventing crime and obtaining public support for what is an intrusive power. I tried to leave people who I had stopped and searched feeling that the police were out to protect them and succeeded in the vast majority of cases. My success rate at finding stolen goods, drugs or weapons was at best one in seven or eight, so explaining my good intentions was essential.

The area covered by Holborn police station ranged from the West End at one end of the patch to Kings Cross in the north. The contrast between these two areas could not be more pronounced, from the glitz of theatre land to the back streets around Euston and Kings Cross railway stations, which were a warren for street prostitutes and minor crime. The prostitutes around Kings Cross in the early 1970s were older women, many of whom had been subject to abuse of one kind and another and a good number who had a heavy reliance on alcohol. As heroin began its remorseless infection of the country the age profile dropped over time to teenagers who were even more desperate. And then there were the ponces, better known by the American slang term 'pimps'. These were young thugs who had targeted girls and forced them into prostitution. They then lived off the girls' earnings and beat them if they didn't earn enough, or had tried to keep some cash back for their own drug problem.

It was on a busy Friday night in August 1972 when I was sitting in the area (emergency response) car, call sign Echo One, opposite Kings Cross railway station and Pancras Way. I was with Dave Jones, the area car driver, a jack-the-lad, but at the same time an instinctive and intuitive policeman. The radio operator was Ken Fergusson, a fellow west country man. I was the plain clothes observer and rookie of the team.

It would be my job to deal with any prisoners, commonly referred to as 'bodies,' we arrested. With only about six months of service I was about to get involved with my first murder. The radio spluttered into life. Information Room (IR) called 'Echo One, Echo One, go to the telephone box in St Pancras Way at the junction with Kings Cross Road and detain the man therein who is on the line to IR.'

It took no longer than thirty seconds to swing our Rover P5 3500 cc automatic into Kings Cross Road, do a short U turn into the east bound carriage way and stop outside a group of phone boxes. I got hold of a man who was speaking into the phone and Ken seized the receiver off him. I didn't know why I had just detained this man; I just did and put him in the police car.

He was very emotional, 'The blood, the blood,' he kept repeating.

Ken returned to the area car and said, 'He's told IR he's killed a prostitute.'

Neither Ken nor Dave were sure he was telling the truth. 'He's a nutter,' one of them said.

Dave and Ken asked him where the body was, he replied, 'It's a blue door.'

This was not a great deal of help as this area of Kings Cross had hundreds of small hotels, a number of which were the haunt of prostitutes and their clients. We drove around in circles for a while, during which time Ken and Dave were still debating if he was mentally ill, or not. Then as we passed 43, Argyle Square, the man, John Kevin Nealon, pointed to a door and said, 'She's in there.' Dave and Ken both went into the small hotel whilst I sat in the back of the police car with Nealon, who was in a highly agitated state.

'She could have been your sister, Jack' he kept saying to me in a northern accent, 'give me a thumping.' He was full of remorse and horror at what he had done. It was later established that the victim was the mother of a minor celebrity of those times who she had abandoned as a baby. This fact was never revealed to the public, and like many other things I learnt in my career about people in the public eye, it remains where it should, locked away for ever.

Dave returned to our car within a couple of minutes, his face was white and taut, 'He has killed a woman, let's get him back to the station.' I arrested Nealon for murder; Ken stayed with the body for evidential reasons and Dave drove swiftly back to the police station, or 'the factory' as it was colloquially known.

When we arrived at Holborn police station I outlined to the sergeant, in Nealon's presence, why we had arrested him. This is a standard procedure and allows the arrested person to hear the reasons for his arrest and challenge them if he is unhappy with the account given. It is the sergeant's responsibility to establish that the constable has exercised legitimate powers of arrest and if appropriate authorise the detention of the arrested person. In this case, not only was the detention authorised, but the sergeant then insisted in writing in great bold capital letters in the detention book (no computers then) the circumstances and names of arresting officers. He was paranoid that the on-duty CID officers would turn up and claim they had arrested the suspect themselves. He seemed to have it in his head that they would fabricate a story and profess to have made the arrest after seeing Nealon in a distressed state in Kings Cross and eliciting the confession by their own dynamic skills. Whether this perception of the sergeant was based on past experience or some exaggerated folk tale I don't know, but he was convinced it was possible. There existed at the time a culture of CID officers taking over arrests from uniform officers and grabbing any kudos themselves. Such practice even had its own phrase – 'body snatching', I was well and truly on Planet Metropolitan Mars.

Nealon appeared eight months later at the Old Bailey where he pleaded not guilty to murder. He claimed that he had been provoked into murdering the prostitute because she had sexually belittled him and kept putting up the price for sex. He confessed that he had lost all reason and strangled her with the chain from a toilet. He admitted that he had descended three floors to the basement, unhooked the chain from the overhead toilet cistern, returned back up the stairs and strangled her. The jury thought this less than spontaneous and returned a verdict of guilty to murder.

The Old Bailey was an imposing place for a young bobby to appear and give evidence. I remember the first day of the trial which was one of great ceremony as it was the opening day of the assize. The judge entered carrying a posy of flowers, an ancient tradition based on the days when Newgate prison was nearby and the scent of the flowers used to combat the stench of the prison. I also had my first taste of the dramatics and histrionics of practiced barristers.

CHAPTER 2

Life on Metpol Mars

I married my first wife, who was from Torquay, Devon, shortly after I joined the Met. We lived in Wilmington Square, Islington and I was able to walk to the police station which was only ten minutes away. It was all very strange for a couple of country bumpkins, but the buzz of the city grew on us. Within a few years we had a baby girl and we moved out of the centre of London to beyond the River Styx to live in Bexleyheath, a suburban area awash with coppers.

The force was almost wholly white at that time, although the canteen staff were almost all West Indian women. We developed a deep affection for 'our staff' and I remember an occasion when a young police cadet of about eighteen spoke down his nose to one of our girls; he was told in no uncertain terms by Dave Jones and other older men to moderate his attitude. The modern world appears to look back on the police in those days as some type of institutionalised racist boy's club organisation. Well, it wasn't like that. Fabrication of evidence – yes; occasional excessive force: – occasionally; institutional racism – no. We lost one of the first black officers to join the Met at Holborn in a road accident just after I joined and the grief was palpable. He was a police officer first and foremost, colour and race didn't come into it, and this was 1971. Whilst I have since heard of very disrespectful and indeed criminal conduct by police officers towards black people, I didn't see any, nor was I aware of any. I worked within a group of about twenty or so constables and sergeants, most of them young like me, I just didn't see any racism, despite later belief that we were all a bunch of bigots. As to being a boy's club, yes it was; but do remember that at this time women were officially paid less than men for doing a similar job. Women were there to deal with female prisoners and children. They were a fraction of the numbers they are now, but they were pretty remarkable women even so.

Homelessness was very much a problem in central London both in the 1970s and sadly it still is today. Central London and particularly the area around Lincoln's Inn Fields appeared a magnet for vagrants and rough sleepers after dark, when the character changed from the sophisticated and elegant workplace for lawyers to a darker dwelling place for the troubled and broken. Rough sleepers in my early days in the police generally tended to be men in their thirties and forties. They were alcoholics, had mental illness and had experienced social upsets such as divorce. They almost exclusively had criminal records and had served sentences of imprisonment. Their harsh lifestyle etched itself upon their faces which frequently bore a map of deep crevasses on weather-beaten leathery skin, with yellow nicotine stains on their fingers. One of my early duties as a beat bobby was to ensure these vagrants were cleared away so that they didn't infect the public highway and were moved on before people arrived at their smart offices in their smart suits the next morning, so a cynical older policeman told me. It was an offence under the Vagrancy Act 1824 to 'wander abroad' – this broadly meant sleeping rough. So, the beat constable would challenge any vagrant sleeping rough as to why they were there and why they were not sleeping in the doss house, or common lodging house as it was officially known. If the said vagrant refused to go to the common lodging house then they could be arrested, not that the station sergeant would thank you very much. In 1971 there were two common lodging houses near my patch, one in Parker Street in Covent Garden and the other, Bruce House, near Drury Lane. These were leftovers from the Victorian age and provided very sparse accommodation, small cubicles and communal showers, but at least they kept people off the streets. With the increase in property prices in central London as well as the gentrification of Covent Garden and other areas of the city, these common lodging houses have disappeared. This social problem has been neglected by successive governments and is a stain on our collective soul; it has been left to church groups and charities to deal with some of our most sick and vulnerable people.

My initial treatment of vagrants as a young policeman was unduly harsh and I was pulled up sharp by an older and wiser officer who said that it could be me on that bench with a bottle of cider in my hand. These people have been screwed up by life he explained. 'It was by chance that they are there and not you.' He was right of course; I was young and arrogant, my deep learning curve continued and I developed the strong social conscience most of us do as we mature.

One such test, which I failed, came when I was called to a disturbance at a hostel for the homeless in the West End, not far from Soho, called Centrepoint. The hippy culture had brought with it the use of LSD and other drugs which resulted in a plague of heroin on our streets. This in turn led to multiple social problems, not least homelessness in the young. When I arrived at the hostel, which was a charity and had not long been set up to try to tackle some of these issues, I was confronted by a bright young man who said that the police were not actually needed anymore as the situation had been resolved. He explained that there had been an episode and a young homeless man had thrown a chair through one of the hostel windows causing some damage. Being a young officer with few arrests under my belt I thought it was a chance to feel someone's collar. The bright young man who was in charge of the hostel was quite insistent that the matter was under control, no complaint was being made and that they would deal with it. I reluctantly agreed, had a cup of tea with the staff and left empty handed. I grew to realise that the police are not just about arresting people, the young man in charge of the hostel had a far better and deeper grip on this problem than I did and once again I was learning fast that there was a lot more grey than black and white in the world. I was told by another colleague who called at the hostel regularly that the young man in charge, to whom I had spoken, was a bright young chap and would go far. His name was Jon Snow and he went into broadcasting and is the news anchor on Channel 4. He remains closely involved with this charity which is known as the New Horizons Youth Centre and continues to help those who are young, homeless and vulnerable.

The IRA commenced their bombing campaign in London in October 1971 when they detonated a bomb in the Post Office Tower in Central London. It went off around 3.00 am, and I happened to be on duty. I was walking the beat in the jewellery centre of Hatton Garden and thought a safe breaker had overestimated the poundage of his explosives. It soon became evident that the true target was the Post Office Tower, a couple of miles away. Fortunately, no one was hurt, but damage had been caused up to 400 yards from the seat of the explosion. This was the extension of a terrorist campaign which had started in Northern Ireland in 1969 and was to claim over three thousand lives. The mainland bombing campaign continued and a year or two later I was on duty in the evening when a car bomb exploded in New Compton Street near Soho, which at the time was beloved of car thieves. I remember we ran out of Holborn police station and stopped a bus. About five constables boarded it and we ordered the driver to take us to Soho which he did. The passengers looked a little concerned, so we apologised for the inconvenience and continued on to our destination. On arrival we rushed to the scene of the explosion where a brick wall of the Telephone Exchange had been demolished. Inside was a black West Indian lady who had been the telephonist on duty. She was dead. Outside was a pile of broken and destroyed motor cars. They were one on top of the other, several at the bottom and one at the very top of the pile. The uppermost vehicle was almost vertical with the boot or trunk pointing skyward. Sticking out of the back window of the car was a child's teddy bear. It looked like a grotesque Christmas tree with the teddy bear taking the place of the angel. And what did the IRA achieve? They killed a West Indian woman who had come to Britain to make a better life for herself and family; she probably barely knew of Ireland.

In the six and a half years I served at Holborn, I only ever once saw police use excessive force. It turned my stomach. I was on night duty working in the front enquiry office dealing with members of the public, who call at the counter to produce their driving documents and other such matters. It was about one in the morning and the station was quiet. The station sergeant was on his meal break and I was in charge of the two or three prisoners we had in the cells, which were along a corridor leading off from the front office where I was working. I heard the sounds of someone in pain or shouting for help, or a combination of the two. I thought perhaps one of the drunks had woken up surprised to find himself in a cell. They do that sometimes, beat the walls and bang their heads against the door and make a complete bloody mess literally. I looked for the cell keys, great large ones similar to those used for the huge doors of a medieval cathedral, but they were missing. Most strange I thought. I coasted down the corridor towards the cells in my Doctor Martins, air soft boots, to see the cell passage and cell doors both open. To my knowledge no one should have been visiting a prisoner without the sergeant's permission and I knew that no such request had been made. I peeped around the iron cell door to see two suited men giving a remorseless kicking to a man writhing on the floor and crying out in pain. I recognised one as a detective sergeant, the other a detective constable. I was mortified, the police were acting like thugs; they were intelligent experienced detectives and I was a mere probationer, completely out of my depth. What should I do?

'Hello, sarge,' I said, 'I heard someone in pain. Shall I call a doctor?'

'No, it's all right son, he'll be alright in a moment.'

I said, 'I'll wait. Do you happen to have the keys?'

They got the message and pushed off, probably a bit worried that a rookie had seen them beating up a prisoner, because a rookie had not been indoctrinated into their perverse culture, one that fortunately was shortly to be called time on. I didn't report it. I suppose I should have, but none of us young recruits were happy with some of the things that were going on around us, and it was our generation that was to change things for the better.

This was the worst police misconduct I saw. I witnessed more frequently the undiluted bravery and service of my colleagues. I stood holding PC Dave Hall's hand in the Royal Free Hospital one night after he had been stabbed just above the heart, whilst in the process of arresting a man for robbing a homosexual in a hotel room; once again, in Kings Cross. This type of crime was considered a lucrative way to get easy cash and was known to criminals as 'rolling a queer'. Dave was a total ladies' man, very handsome and charming. At one point, he thought he was dying and he said to me, 'I'm going, Tony.' He later told me that when he thought he was dying he was inwardly lamenting all the women that he had not had sex with! His life was saved by a young doctor no more than twenty-three years old – but looked sixteen – and some dedicated nurses.

It wasn't all murder and mayhem, although sometimes the mayhem was self-induced. Once when working as the jailer I assisted the station sergeant in charging a vagrant with being drunk and incapable. After he had sobered up, his personal property was returned to him. It comprised old newspapers, cigarette papers, tobacco and sundry items. He scooped it all off the charge room table and into the voluminous pockets of an old army great coat he was wearing and he left the station. About half an hour later I looked for the cell keys to give the half a dozen or so miscreants in custody their usual hourly check. I couldn't find the keys in their usual place and asked the sergeant if he had them, but he hadn't. This was serious; it was immediately serious because I guarded them like the crown jewels since my experience with the CID beating up a man in my custody. We checked to see if any officer had recently visited a prisoner; no one had. In fact, the last action to take place was to release the vagrant. No, surely not! It dawned on the sergeant and me simultaneously; the vagrant had stolen the keys in an almighty act of spite. The sergeant, losing his reason, ran to the radio console and sent a message to all officers in a wavering voice to track down and show no mercy to the vagabond suspected of theft of the cell keys. A constable passing through the radio room helpfully suggested he phone the fire brigade to break down all six cell doors to release the prisoners who were effectively trapped inside. The sergeant, who was purple with rage by now, almost strangled him. Five minutes or so later, both the sergeant and I walked to the front public enquiry counter having come from the radio room checking every possible nook and cranny for the keys. We were both on our knees searching under the counter when we heard the front door to the station open and close. There, standing before us in all his magnificence, was the tramp, woollen great coat ruffled, hair ruffled, in fact everything was ruffled including us.

'I found these in my pockets. Are they yours? I don't recognise them.'

He slid two large cell keys, a heavy chain and other vital station keys across the counter towards us. We could have kissed him – but didn't. The sergeant whose career was now back on track, and saved from ignominy, handed the bewildered fellow a one pound note to enjoy a slap-up breakfast, which he did and the Metropolitan Police survived for another day.

After six happy years at the Met and due to some family problems, I applied to transfer back home, but the Devon and Cornwall Constabulary was at full strength and not recruiting. So I applied to join the Avon and Somerset Constabulary, the county next door. One of the reasons I gave when interviewed was that I wanted to have a fresh start nearer home because my marriage had experienced a problem. Unfortunately, this was just not what the Avon and Somerset Police wanted to hear and I fell spectacularly on my face when interviewed and I was adjudged too toxic to handle. Not to be daunted, I got the map out and located the next available county along the coast from Devon which happened to be Dorset. I had only ever passed through Dorset on my way to London. It had a long coast line and largish towns; it would do, but this time I thought it wise not to mention my domestic disasters.

CHAPTER 3

Wessex

On 3 May 1976, I started life as a uniformed constable in Dorset. This was the time of the Ted Heath government with countless strikes by coal miners and factory car workers; the country was on its knees. I was posted to Weymouth which is a lovely Georgian town with a beautiful beach and as I walked along the sea front in full uniform I had to pinch myself to believe I was actually being paid for this. 'Don't go breaking my heart' by Elton John and Kiki Dee blasted out from every pub. Life was quieter than London and I missed the buzz. Weymouth, like many towns in Dorset, has a close community which tended to look in on itself. If you asked anybody in Weymouth had they read the paper that day, they would usually reply, 'The *Echo* hasn't arrived yet.' The only newspaper worth reading in Weymouth was the local *Dorset Echo*; what happened outside Weymouth wasn't worth knowing about and may as well have been on the dark side of the moon.

I spent a couple of years as a uniformed constable, getting used to some different policing methods. Dorset in those days had some cumbersome bureaucratic report-writing procedures which seemed to involve writing the same thing at least three times. Fortunately, this withered as the pace of life and rate of crime increased exponentially. I was a dab hand at arresting felons in London for possessing heroin, frequently surprising them in underground toilets where they would go to 'jack up'. However, in 1976 in Weymouth I could find not one heroin user, mainly because there weren't any, not the street variety at least. Sadly, this was to change over the years as this destructive plague spread from the cities.

In 1977, I entered the mysterious world of the CID as a trainee detective where I would have to prove myself if I wanted to become a detective constable. The CID was a reclusive and exclusive organisation in those days, sometimes referred to as 'the family' in more sinister terms than it deserved. Once again good fortune put me in the right place at the right time and I was assigned a case involving a local fisherman who was stealing crab pots from other fishermen. This may sound small beer to a city dweller, but it is almost a capital crime in a fishing community as it amounts to the bread being stolen out of other men's mouths. Crab pots aren't cheap either and are time-consuming to make. The steel wire frame in those days' cost about £25 and then needed old strips of rubber wound around them, and weights to hold it down, as well as long lengths of rope. A 'string' of twenty-five pots would cost about £625 and most fishermen needed about six to ten strings to work. So with the cost of the boat and equipment, fishing had a reasonably high start-up cost. The suspect, Nick Jacks, didn't have the money for this kind of outlay so resorted to stealing the other fishermen's pots. I spoke to a number of fishermen who had lost pots and started to build a picture of our man, and it was clear the fishing community were giving the police (me) an ultimatum. Either we get him, or if we didn't, the fishermen would. These guys were a tough bunch; they were used to hard physical work in dangerous conditions and are extremely physically fit. They also tipped me the nod that he was receiving stolen equipment, mainly expensive rope and other marine equipment, from the Royal Navy stores at HM Naval Base Portland – somewhat of a local pastime.

Jacks was a tough chap with arms like tree trunks. He had the foulest mouth I have ever come across, and I often heard him swearing and shouting at other fishermen as he set out to sea from Weymouth harbour during our observations. Together with another rookie detective we maintained surveillance on Jacks as he set out daily in his small fishing boat to 'shoot' crab pots at various locations off Portland, not usually more than a mile from the shore line. We drove along the coastal paths around 'the island' in my old Ford Escort Mark 2 almost knocking the bottom out of it on the rugged terrain. We stopped at various points on the cliff tops to spy on him through binoculars. It took us a month of continual observations involving very early starts through a glorious summer to amass the evidence needed. I managed to log all the points where he dropped crab pots and so after several weeks, I had plotted and taken compass bearings of all his fishing marks. Our break came four weeks into the job. He came out of Weymouth harbour and turned left (east) towards Lulworth Cove. Normally he sailed west to the fishing marks off Portland. About two hours later he re-appeared steaming straight back to Portland, where off 'Chene House' he shot a line of pots. Interestingly enough, the buoys at each end of the 'string' had triangular red flags. A quick check was made with local fishermen and I was told that the Miller family from Lulworth Cove mark all their pots with flags. I phoned Mr Miller and sure enough he had had a string of pots stolen. He came over to Portland some hours later and met me; together with our colleagues in the Ministry of Defence Police we set out to sea in their launch. We sailed out to where we had seen the pots being laid and drew one up. Mr Miller was adamant they were his; he recognised the way they were bound with old rubber. We dropped the pot back into the sea and took a written statement regarding the theft from our victim. It was a sixteen-hour day and this would be the shape of things to come.

Early the next day, my colleague waited on the cliffs by Chene House; I was down in Portland dockyard on the MOD launch. At about 9 am a couple of hours after Jacks had set sail from Weymouth, he was seen by my colleague approaching Mr Miller's pots. I received confirmation of his position by radio and the skipper of our boat set off in pursuit. As we rounded the headland into Chene Bay I saw Jacks working one of the last pots in the line with his crewman, a crab pot attached to a buoy with a flag on it lay on the deck. I was wearing a Harris Tweed sports coat, bought by me especially for the occasion of working on the CID.

I shouted from the MOD launch, 'Mr Jacks?'

He replied, 'Yes,' and looked a little puzzled as I had the cut of a land lubber whilst the crew on the launch were all kitted out with life jackets and boating clothing.

'Alright if I come aboard?'

'Yeah, okay,' he replied, somewhat bemused and I unsteadily crossed from the launch to the fishing smack.

I walked along the deck towards Jacks who gave me a smile and said, 'Want a tea?'

I noticed he was holding a broad bladed knife about nine inches long. He was nipping the claws of the crabs, which is to cut the tendons on their claws, before throwing them into a box. He towered above me in an apron with his shirt sleeves cut at the biceps to give his muscular arms more room. Now was the time for sheer face. 'Whose pots are these?' I asked firmly.

'Mine,' he said, 'who's asking?'

I replied 'I'm PC Nott from Weymouth police station; you nicked these from Miller at Lulworth yesterday. You're under arrest,' and I gave him the full caution. 'Turn this boat around and sail back to Portland.'

His face dropped, eyes screwed up into two slits and he stared at me, he pushed the knife forward and said, 'Keep away from me.'

I just repeated, 'Turn the boat around and return to Portland.'

I looked across at the MOD launch; it had drifted twenty feet away from the fishing smack. The crew were all looking at me and I could almost hear them thinking, 'What's going to happen next?' Great, I thought.

To my amazement, and due only to my acting abilities to appear tough and confident, the knife-wielding giant threw the remaining pots overboard and turned his boat towards Portland Harbour. Jacks' teenage son was also on board and I started talking to him.

'Keep away from him, you bastard,' shouted Jacks and there followed a string of abuse about my parentage and sexual inadequacies as a man.

I approached him at the stern where he was standing at the boat's wheel; he fondled the knife, which resembled a small cutlass.

'Look, Mr Jacks,' (I was very polite) 'we've got to sort this out. I know what you've been up to, as do most of the fishermen in Weymouth; it's time to come clean.'

'Those bastards' and other non-complimentary remarks about the local fishing community issued forth from his large mouth like a gushing torrent.

'Yes, look, I know you're hard working, I've seen you working like a galley slave, but you can't be stealing everybody else's pots.'

'Where are they then?' he quizzically asked.

'We'll talk about that back at the station, and we'd better go to your lock up store on the way and get back all that pussers' [purser or RN logistics officer] rope while we're at it; I've been watching you for weeks.'

Jacks could see the game was up; it was clear to him that I knew all about his movements. Over the next few days we recovered about two hundred crab pots which we stored in the police garages at Weymouth police station. They had all been baited with mackerel which was secured inside each pot. In my excitement at such a large haul of stolen goods I forgot to have the bait removed. After about a week the whole station environs and houses round about stank of rotten fish. I had taken some days off after the end of the job so when I got back to work the station was literally buzzing or should I say humming with the smell which had infected the locality. I said rather innocently "I wonder if it's those crab pots I put in the garages?" This rookie detective ended up on the carpet of Chief Superintendent McPherson; he was an old Scots war hero who had won the Military Cross for charging a German machine gun nest in Crete. After my admonishment, he laughed at my serious countenance and said, 'Never ye mind lad, the harder you work the more likely you are to drop clangers,' or less polite words to that effect.

Jacks' boat was later sunk by some fishermen when it was moored at Weymouth harbour mainly because he got a suspended prison sentence and the judge failed to grasp the impact of this crime on the local community. I later acquired information which led me to arrest a number of local fishermen who were running around in their boats with state-of-the-art navigation equipment stolen from Portland Naval Base. These were Decca Mark 21 devices found on the bridges of destroyers and worth then about £25,000 apiece. I recovered four of them from different boats. They were like modern satnavs which now go for £50 but in the mid-seventies this was virtually top-secret kit. Jacks packed up fishing and became a successful road haulier and business man. He was also a good welder, and partly by way of showing me he didn't mean all those things he'd said about my mother and my lack of a father, he welded the floor in my rusting Ford Escort Mk 2 and advised me to get rid of it as soon as possible before I killed myself. He was a hard-working chap who had gone into business without sufficient capital, and I grew to like the rough, foul-mouthed giant.

CHAPTER 4

A Rookie Detective

Shortly after I had arrested Jacks, I found myself being permanently established as a detective constable in Weymouth. This came a little to my surprise because for some time another lad had been tipped for the post but had got intoxicated one night and threatened to punch the detective sergeant's lights out, which was not a career-enhancing move. As well as settling my future to a life in the Criminal Investigation Department, I became used to a regular diet of fresh crabs, which I frequently found on the steps of Portland police station scratching around inside a box with my name on it.

Dorset is a 'family' force and in Weymouth I met men who were to weave in and out of my life. Dave King was an ambitious detective constable whose desk was always a mess of papers which gave the intentional impression that he was the hardest working guy in the office. He eventually made detective chief superintendent. Martin Holloway, another detective constable, was to be my best man when I married for the second time. Martin was a rugby player who regularly accompanied CID social events with his skills on the guitar and repertoire of folk ballads. His nickname was the Ayatollah on account of his travels in Iran. Martin was also a career detective; later he was to take on the sombre task of being the senior identification officer for the many victims of the Boxing Day Thailand Tsunami in 2004, before retiring as a detective chief inspector. The CID office was full of such colourful characters. We were watched over by Detective Sergeant Derrick Penny who was the steady hand in the office and held it all together. He was a bespectacled, taciturn man, more of a thinker than an action man, serious and safe. Pete Harrison the other detective sergeant of the duo, was a huge chap, built like a tank, and later to be my boss in Bournemouth; he had an enormous sense of humour and a great belly-rumbling laugh.

Having been accepted into the CID I was posted to Portland police station where I was the sole detective constable. The uniformed constables, one per shift, worked from six in the morning until two; from two in the afternoon until ten in the evening; and then ten to six the following morning. There were two 'home beat' officers who lived on the island which brought the compliment of officers to six. In 2010, due to the recession and reduction of police budgets, the police station was closed and all the officers were transferred out. The magistrates court, which adjoined the police station, also closed down in a bid to centralise services and cut costs. Portland, like many other communities throughout the country lost any real semblance of true community policing and was covered thereafter from Weymouth when something had grown into an emergency. Even here the police station close to the shops and sea front was closed and relocated to an industrial estate on the fringe of the town.

The island – although Portland is in fact connected to the mainland by a road over a bridge across the Fleet Lagoon – is the jewel in Dorset's crown, projecting out into the sea like a lozenge-shaped pendant in the south of the county. It is peppered with old quarries, from the days when Sir Christopher Wren took stone for St Paul's Cathedral and other buildings in London and it now boasts a busy port which formerly belonged to the Royal Navy. The 'islanders' are a proud and independent breed who view people from off the island as foreigners – 'they'm baint one o'we' – and people who move there to live, but can't claim to have been born there, are reduced to the rank of 'Kimberlins'. I would regularly get phone calls from officers in various city forces requesting I visit inmates at the Borstal and prison which were situated on the island.

'What's the weather like down there, mate?' I would frequently be asked.

'Oh, not bad,' I would say, 'I can see the mackerel boats bobbing up and down about half a mile away as my office overlooks the sea, and the girls in their bikinis are a bit of a distraction, but I soldier on.'

I was frequently called a lucky illegitimate son of a gun or something similar as my city colleagues drooled over my descriptions. Portland was like going back in time. Shopkeepers in the main street always left their goods on display outside their shops when they went for their lunch. When they returned everything was as they left it, other than probably a customer waiting for the shop keeper to return and pay for an item. People would boast of leaving their doors unlocked and still do. Crime tended to be very local, and I had some mighty strange cases to deal with. One involved a Portlander who had stolen another Portlander's rowing boat and revenge was extracted by the thief's goat being hung from a tree. On another occasion, I dealt with a man for incest with his daughter and whose only other conviction was for bestiality!

As a young detective constable, I started to gain experience in the murky world of police informants. In those days there were no courses or even much in the way of instructions in the use of these much-needed crime investigation resources. The usual way of recruiting informants was to encourage people under arrest, to give you information once their court case or prison sentence had been concluded. Frequently, information would be passed to you after their arrest and prior to conviction, in the hope that it would reduce the length of their sentence. One such informant I had was Charlie Bramble, a half-baked Portland resident, with a sharp pointed face and swarthy complexion reminiscent of a weasel. He had a penchant for conning money out of people on the promise of mending their car. He never properly mended or serviced their car, just got drunk on the money, sold the car to somebody else, then repeated the whole process again. He was a complete menace; his only redeeming feature was that he offered me information about local criminals. I was quite excited to register my first informant, who told me the identity of a man who was responsible for a burglary in a hotel.

I arrested the miscreant who denied the burglary in question although he admitted some other offences of minor theft. He told me he would admit the burglary if I gave him bail, but he didn't seem to know a great deal about how the crime was committed. I had some misgivings and went back to the hotel to check out more details of the burglary. Whilst there I was told that another detective had called earlier to make the same enquiries. I went back to the CID office to discover that a colleague of mine was dealing with another person also locked up at Weymouth police station for a string of hotel burglaries including the one I was investigating. The other prisoner was, however, able to give the ins and outs of how he had committed the crime for which I had got an admission from my man. Clearly my suspect had only admitted the burglary to get bail. This lesson taught me three things: never ever use the chance of giving bail to a criminal as an inducement to make a confession (any such admission is inadmissible in law anyway); two, always test confessions against facts known only to the offender; and three, always treat information from informants with the greatest of care.

The use of informants is usually the most cost-effective and efficient way of investigating crime and they offer information for a variety of reasons. One informant I ran successfully for many years gave me information leading to the recovery of hundreds of thousands of pounds' worth of drugs and property. He was a former armed robber and wanted to pay back society for the crimes he had committed. However, a small number of informants can have their own devious reasons. Bramble was a Walter Mitty type who only avoided being strangled because I couldn't immediately lay my hands upon him.

It was at this stage when life seemed to be very good with lots of prospects and a frequent diet of crabs, that my marriage took a turn for the worse leading eventually to a divorce. Thankfully my parents were prepared to help with the children. Initially I was going to resign and move with the children to my parent's home in Devon. I was prepared to sweep the streets rather than lose my children, but they insisted I stay in the Dorset Police and they would move to Dorset and live with me. I did not keep it all to myself this time but told my friends and colleagues straight away. I stood up on parade the day after the breakup and announced what had happened to my friends and colleagues, told them my mum and dad would look after the children and I was okay. I didn't need anything from them other than the odd whiskey put in my direction from time to time.

One Sunday morning a few months earlier I had been allocated a job by DS Penny. 'You can deal with this, Notty,' he said. 'Someone over at Portland's carved their husband up. You can speak their language, have a look at it.'

I was handed a bundle of papers in which a local man had been taken to hospital late the previous evening having been sliced up with a razor knife or box cutter. He had received a number of stitches and had been released back to his home on Portland. His wife was locked up in the cells at Weymouth, but the husband had not made a written statement of complaint. One problem with domestic violence is that a written statement was at this time required from the injured party. Sometimes, the victim is in too much fear of their spouse to make a statement and they just don't want the police involved. However, I was a constable of about seven or eight years' service and I knew well that seventy five per cent of all murders are domestic related and unless I took positive action it could well happen again. I set off for Portland from Weymouth police station, intent on getting a statement.

When I arrived at the house it was like someone had died. The injured man's mother was a very dominant and over-emotional woman. She was cussing and shaking her fist in the air at the mention of her son's wife. She didn't want the police there and the injured man sat in a chair saying nothing, wrapped in bandages. I asked him if he would make a statement to which he quietly and firmly said, 'No.' His mother howled in rage, did some kind of war dance and then tripped over, landing on the edge of the settee. This was wholly out of proportion to the events which had occurred. Whilst seriously hurt, he was still alive and appeared to be able to make a full recovery. I looked at the antics of the mother and I am sorry to admit such a terrible thing, but I almost lost it. For no apparent reason I wanted to laugh at the lunacy being performed in front of me. It got so bad

I laughed out loud then immediately started coughing and explained I had a cold. My eyes were streaming with tears, but not from grief and I think I got away with it. I duly left the family with no statement and no case. As I left, I made an enquiry with people nearby one of whom was the dream of a young woman. Deep brown eyes like bottomless pools, slim figure, good legs, full lips. Yes, it was love at first sight and I made sure to keep her phone number. Fortune was again good to me that day.

When I got back to the station, I told DS Penny that I didn't have a case. 'Well, Tone, we can't have Her Majesty's citizens carving each other up and not accounting for it. Better have a word with the wife; if she coughs it you can charge her.' I duly interviewed the suspect which was a straight one-to-one question and answer session later recorded by me into my pocket book and all that was necessary in those days. I didn't mention that I hadn't got a statement from her husband, but she obligingly admitted slicing her husband up after an argument about her going clubbing. She made a full statement under caution, went to court and pleaded guilty the next day to the Magistrates. I learned a big lesson from this case, and from then on would more often than not make arrests in domestic violence cases and charge the offender whenever I could. I would never risk letting violent partners off the hook. My nightmare was to fail to take positive action in a domestic violence case and find that the partner had later been killed by their spouse. The police have wide powers to arrest a person to prevent a breach of the peace and take that person before a magistrate to have them bound over to be of good behaviour. It is a good mechanism to prevent violent husbands assaulting their wives and does not necessitate the injured party making a statement or appearing in court. This authority has its origins back in 1361 and is contained in the Justice of the Peace Act. I used this power on many occasions.

After my wife had left me with the children, and giving it a polite time gap, I dug out the old crime file concerning the domestic violence case and found the telephone number of the lithe girl I had met nearby. I asked her out and to my surprise she accepted. Judith and I were married a couple of years later and Martin Holloway was my best man. Things continued to improve as almost simultaneously, I was promoted to detective sergeant and posted to Boscombe, a run-down part of Bournemouth, twenty-five miles away.

Chapter 5

Reported Missing:
The Case of Peter Taylor Part One

I moved to Boscombe in March 1982, just as the Falklands war broke out. Margaret Thatcher was the Prime Minister and she displayed unflinching leadership which led to the recovery of the Falkland Islands and the increase of Britain's prestige in the world. However, her later uncompromising approach to the miners, during the strike of 1984–85, polarised public opinion, which in turn made my life difficult as my future mother-in-law was the daughter of a Yorkshire miner. Enough said.

Boscombe was a once fashionable Edwardian suburb of Bournemouth which experienced a period of decline as its elegance faded. It is about three miles east of the good quality shops, plush apartment blocks and hotels of central Bournemouth. Boscombe has a main shopping street of its own, with expensive houses towards Christchurch and the sea and some good hotels and guest houses. Around the main shopping thoroughfare are side streets of graceful Edwardian houses with ornate balconies. Sadly, many of these have been divided into flats, and were during the 1980s occupied by a flotsam of mainly young men from Liverpool and Manchester. Whilst many of these were honest, upright people looking for work in the hotel trade, a number were not, being drug dealers, pimps and general thieves. With good quality housing and people of some substance at one end of the patch, and a cloud of loose-knit scoundrels at the other with a sprinkling of local villains to add variety, the mix was present for some exciting coppering.

Boscombe police station was a small sub-station to Bournemouth with a complement of eight detective constables, two detective sergeants and about forty uniformed patrol officers. We were all responsible for this patch and due to this localised form of policing I don't think many villains escaped our combined attention. The crime rate was high, in part due to the character of the patch, but the detection rate was correspondingly good.

Being promoted to sergeant is probably one of the biggest leaps you make in the police. I was not quite management nor was I 'one of the lads'. It is necessary to enforce discipline without alienating yourself from those who are key to the job, the men and women who do the work. I made an immediate bad impression and was perceived as a boy from the country – i.e. Weymouth – by the big city boys of Boscombe. In the rural west of the county I was used to detective constables attending crime scenes, interviewing witnesses and sometimes suspects on their own. I had worked in Portland on my own and not infrequently arrested suspects on my own; so why did some of the detectives at Boscombe insist on going every-where hand in hand? After one or two heated rows, and in one case tears, things settled down and we all got used to each other. I was very fortunate to work with an older and more experienced detective sergeant, Steve Maidment, who I would later work with on a number of major crimes. Steve was a highly competent detective who had a flash of electric energy in everything he did. The station cleaner, a lovely woman, was besotted with him and spent more time cleaning our office when he was there than any other part of the police station.

A couple of weeks after my arrival in March 1982, I heard the name Peter Taylor for the first time. I was sitting in the detective sergeant's office at Boscombe police station wading through the usual mountain of crime reports, when a young constable, Steve 'Beaker' Coombes, walked into the office with a file under his arm. He was a smart young man, hair immaculately groomed, black, straight and short. He wore the standard police uniform, jacket with a Dorset Police badge on the left breast, rather like a sheriff's badge, with no epaulettes. His uniform trousers had creases as sharp as a knife blade.

'Hi, Beaker,' I said, taking the pipe out of my mouth and lounging back in my smart office chair.

'Hello, sarge,' he said, and then commenced to tell me a story about a woman who had gone missing about five days previously. Her name was Monica Taylor; she was aged fifty-two and lived at the Costa del Sol hotel, Sea Road, Boscombe. She had been married for twenty-seven years to Peter Taylor, a hotelier by occupation, but was now separated from him, pending a divorce. She lived in a holiday apartment within the block whilst he ran the remainder as summer lets. They had three children, a son living in Venezuela with his girlfriend, and two daughters who both lived away. Mrs. Taylor was reported missing to the police by one of her daughters after she had failed to meet her father in Bournemouth the previous Saturday (3 April 1982) a ritual they both strictly observed. She had also failed to keep a 10.30 am appointment at her hairdressers, 'Luigi's', the day before. Steve Coombes had done a thorough job; he also established that Mrs. Taylor was looking forward to a trip to Venezuela to visit her son. It now seemed to be a matter for the CID as Steve, being a uniformed officer, could not devote the time needed to this investigation, as his job was one of patrolling the beat within a strict shift pattern. He handed to me all the messages and circulations he had made in an effort to find Mrs Taylor, as well as the missing person file. I looked through the colloquially named misper file and noticed that Steve had kept a meticulous record of his enquiries. In it he had noted the names and phone numbers of family members he had spoken to, plus shop owners and neighbours. In the file was a photograph of Monica Taylor; she was an elegant woman with shoulder length dark hair, with an innocent smile on her face.

I reported up through my chain of command to my detective inspector and told him about the missing person case which I had now taken on. Detective Inspector Lumbard was a taciturn, professional detective with a proven track record of investigations. My first task was to visit the scene of the disappearance which I did in company with the DI. We called on Mrs Leo, a neighbour who had the key to Monica's flat and then went with her to the apartment at the Costa del Sol. We found the flat exactly as it had been left when Monica was reported missing, and which had not been touched by Mrs. Leo. The front door was locked and undamaged, and could only be opened with the key, which Mrs Leo supplied. All doors and windows were intact and locked. The light for the electric fire in the lounge was on, all the curtains were drawn open, and the flat was in immaculate order. The bed was made, and there were items of jewellery on the dressing table together with some photographs of her family. Some family photographs were also on the bed. I found a note pad on the dining room table which had written '28216 7.41 £13.10'. Checks made later with British Rail revealed this to be a fast train to London operating on Saturdays and Sundays and the corresponding return fare. There were also shopping and 'to do' lists on the table. One shopping list included 'Disprins' which was crossed off but other items on the list were not.

The only thing out of place in this immaculate apartment were some dirty dishes in the sink including an egg cup, dinner plate, cutlery and drinking glass; the remains of a boiled egg were on the draining board. Mrs. Leo felt that Monica was such a tidy person that she must have disappeared very shortly after the dishes were put into the sink. In the refrigerator were two pints of milk with codes on the tops. I established that her milk was supplied by a local dairy, who later confirmed that they had been delivered on Thursday 1 and Friday 2 April. It seemed that we could pin the time of her disappearance down to somewhere between 8 am and 10.30 am (Luigi's) on the Friday. No trace could be found of any Disprins, nor indeed empty containers for them. The question was, what had happened?

We next saw Monica's estranged husband Peter, a pleasant and congenial man who lived in a separate apartment at the Costa del Sol. He was about five feet ten inches tall, medium to muscular build with straight black hair, parted to one side. He appeared quiet, genial and helpful and gave an aura of being unconcerned and was certainly not nervous. He informed us that his wife had a fragile mental state and had twice before attempted to commit suicide. He admitted that she was a sensitive, genteel woman who probably couldn't take the divorce. He then went on to describe the first suicide attempt by Monica, which had occurred two years previously. He heard her shouting his name from her apartment in a distressed state. He went to find her and enquire as to the problem and she confessed to him that she had taken a number of sedatives. Almost immediately she coughed up vomit wherein could be seen some undigested tablets. He called an ambulance and she was admitted to hospital where she received treatment for an overdose. She was then transferred to a local psychiatric hospital, where after a period of around a month she was discharged and received outpatient care under a psychiatrist.

Her last attempt to kill herself had been almost a year before she was reported missing. Peter Taylor believed that this was only an attempt at attention seeking, as she was becoming more bitter about their impending divorce. She was not taken to hospital and he felt it was a lot less serious. In the first attempt, he told us that she had taken 200 Disprins. On that occasion, family photographs had been left scattered on the bed, which no doubt she had been gazing at as she slipped into unconsciousness. I was able to later corroborate this information with other family members.

He also added that the disappearance of his wife would complicate the divorce proceedings, as she would not be around to sign certain legal papers and he could lose out financially. We politely asked if we could search around the Costa del Sol complex which we did in a cursory manner. The hotel had been divided into holiday apartments and had undergone considerable rebuilding and renovation; Mr Taylor was a hard-working practical man, who had undertaken a lot of the building work himself. To search the apartments properly would have needed a small army, as well as more than mere suspicion to submit an innocent citizen to that level of scrutiny. I also checked his small disused petrol filling station further along Sea Road with the same negative result. He was unable to give any suggestions as to where she may have gone.

Monica had devoted her life to her family and did not have a wide circle of friends. When a detective enters into an investigation it is always important to make background checks into the people you are engaged in dealing with. As a matter of routine, I wanted to know if the astute hard-working businessman and hotelier before me had any other sides to his character. Accordingly, therefore, I checked his name with the Criminal Records Office and found that he had a couple of convictions in the 1950s involving handling stolen motor vehicles, but nothing since. Whilst not damning in itself, it opened up an aspect of his character which was useful to know about.

Through the help of Mrs. Leo, Monica's solicitor was traced and visited. He explained that Monica had been quite depressed in the past when she had first visited him. However, as time went by, she became resigned to the necessity of a divorce and her mental strength had increased. There had been detailed legal proceedings before the County Court and her solicitor noticed that she was becoming quite formidable. Due to Mr Taylor's failure to produce all his financial documents, a hearing had been arranged for Wednesday 7 April; owing to her disappearance however, the case did not proceed.

I made a number of routine enquiries which were standard in a case like this. I obtained further photographs of her which I circulated through the local press; checks were made with her bank, building society, insurance agent, dentist and doctor, but all drew blanks. She was close to her father, sister, and children but they all had heard nothing; she had simply dropped off the planet. Her flight to visit her son in Venezuela had been booked for 15 April but had not been paid for. Friends of hers who I traced and visited during the course of enquiries believed that Monica had abandoned hope of going, as she had not received the fare for the ticket from her son. He was later seen and explained that his mother did not appreciate the time it took for correspondence to travel from England to Venezuela and back again. It was suggested by one family member that this and her displeasure with one of her daughter's boyfriends could have made her depressed. This and the anniversary of her previous suicide attempts seemed to be pointing to suicide; not forgetting the family photographs spread on the bed.

DI Lumbard called on the psychiatrist who treated Monica on her previous suicide attempts and outlined the case of

Monica's disappearance to him. The psychiatrist thought that taken with the potentially missing Disprins, the cancelled trip to Venezuela and her previous mental state that suicide was the most likely option. I submitted the 'Missing Person' file to my senior officers for review and instructions and it was returned with the official view that it was a probable suicide.

As time wore on however, I became increasingly worried that this conclusion was wrong. None of Monica's clothes or suitcases were missing from her flat and I continued to take statements from her friends and relatives. The constant theme was that she had become much more formidable. Yes, she had been driven to attempting suicide by the divorce, she had been frantic and in a state of complete shock by her husband's affair with a much younger woman, but she was getting over it. Her solicitor made a detailed statement which clearly illustrated how Monica had become far stronger and had helped meticulously in the pre-financial hearing preparations. She had identified omissions from accounting books, formerly produced by her husband, which showed lower receipts than she knew had been made. She also had forced him into admitting that a flat in Spain belonged to him and was not rented as he had claimed. In fact, Monica was pushing for full possession of the Costa del Sol hotel which would have left Peter getting the garage site in Sea Road and the flat in Spain. This is something he would find hard to countenance, especially since he had worked so hard to build up the business. This was looking like a motive for murder.

From neighbours and friends, I established that Peter Taylor had met a Venezuelan girl much younger than himself about five years before and who was related to the wife of his son. The affair developed into a full-blown relationship which resulted in Peter living with her at the Costa del Sol hotel, and Monica moving into another apartment in the same complex. This had been the cause of the first and second suicide attempts. In mid-May of that year I went back to see Peter Taylor again. I started by talking generally about his wife, and of any news he may have had about her. He told me that he had heard nothing, and that he believed his wife was alive and living somewhere but keeping her head down to cause him problems. He said that if the divorce was not settled, then he would have to wait seven years before she could be declared dead. In that time, his girlfriend's visa might not be renewed and she could be deported to Venezuela. He also estimated that his assets were worth £120,000 and he was prepared to offer Monica half. He was adamant that he would not sell or lose the Costa del Sol, which he had turned from an old hotel into good quality holiday apartments, with his own hands. He was once again very charming and helpful.

I checked out the issue regarding deportation of the girlfriend with the Immigration Department and was told that it was unlikely she would be deported in the circumstances. Apparently, she would have been allowed to stay as a 'foreign mistress'. The generous approach of Mr Taylor to a financial settlement, as he had so pleasantly told me, was really the very opposite from what I discovered within the documents and her affidavit in the legal proceedings currently under way. Legally he was fighting it all the way.

Later that same month I got an unexpected bonus when I called on Mrs Leo for a chat about Monica. She produced a large bag of correspondence which Monica had given her for safekeeping. The papers included her full affidavit covering the current divorce and financial hearings, and personal diaries. These painted an entirely different picture of the genial Peter Taylor I had met. The diaries listed assaults on her by Peter and his mistress; intimidation to make her move by taking her belongings from her flat and leaving them outside in the hallway; as well as the placing of a dead rat in one of her cupboards. She suspected Peter had a door key and was entering her apartment and searching through her belongings. I followed up the domestic violence and traced her doctor who had retired. He confirmed that she had complained of injuries following assaults on her by Peter. The placing of the dead rat in her cupboard was also confirmed by her solicitor to whom she had reported that incident. The problem, however, was that at this time, much of this was regarded in law as 'hearsay' and was not admissible in court, as it was not said in the presence and hearing of the defendant. The next two years passed with no body being found. I continued to see Monica's father who never gave up and went through terrible times as a result of his beloved daughter's disappearance as did her sister, Mrs. Horlock.

Among the papers recovered from Mrs Leo were a full set of accounts for the running of the business at the Costa del Sol hotel. They were in fact the correct accounts for the business and not the fraudulent accounts Peter had submitted to the Inland Revenue, and Monica made it clear that he had been 'cooking the books' in her diaries. Somehow the correct accounts found their way into the hands of the Inland Revenue who established from the new figures that an underpayment of £28,000 had been made in one year alone. The new tax bill he received annoyed him greatly, but it didn't bring us any closer to finding out what had happened to Monica.

CHAPTER 6

Fate Plays A Hand:
The Case of Peter Taylor Part Two

1984 was an eventful year; the great struggle took place between Arthur Scargill, the leader of the coal miners and the Prime Minister, Margaret Thatcher, which saw the eventual destruction of the coal mining industry. Madonna released 'Like a Virgin' and the IRA concluded the year with the bombing of the Grand Hotel in Brighton, killing five men and women and seriously injuring a number of others; Margaret Thatcher was lucky to escape uninjured. I got married in August to Judith who had a son from her previous marriage. We all started to learn the pleasures and difficulties of a second marriage, in which both partners have with them their human bundles from their former relationship, just to make their lives together even more interesting.

Promotion to detective sergeant was not just about investigating more serious and complex crime, it was about supervision and management. I tended to be protective and respectful of women, but slow to change in the rapidly changing world of equality. In the late '70s and early '80s girlie calendars adorned the walls of many CID offices alongside mug shots of various wanted villains and descriptions of stolen property and the like. I saw nothing wrong with it; after all the national gallery was full of paintings of naked women! Boscombe CID office was no different. Then an edict came down from headquarters that all such girlie calendars should be taken down; such behaviour was no longer acceptable. It seemed to me like iconoclasm, the Reformation indeed. All this art work was to be destroyed, all for some politically correct whim. One of the detectives told me that headquarters were now demanding that all such pictures be removed, so I cast myself as some kind of King Canute, misjudged the moment completely and said the calendar could stay.

A couple of weeks later I was working in my office, which was separate to the main detective constables' office, wading through the usual mountain of paperwork. A young uniformed policewoman came into my office and asked to have a word. There was no one in the main office; the rest of the lads were out and we were alone. I was expecting her to ask me for some advice on a crime she was investigating, but she said to me that there was something which was upsetting her. She then continued that yesterday she was in the main CID office talking to one of the detectives when she saw the calendar. It made her so upset she lost track of what she was talking about and described how she was overcome with humiliation. I noticed her eyes were becoming pink with a very light covering of water. It had taken her a lot of courage to approach me and she was again upset. 'I didn't know,' I told her and floundered unconvincingly. 'Those things shouldn't be there. How has that happened?' I asked to no one in particular. 'I will see it comes down. There's no place for anything like that in the modern Dorset Police,' I added. I thanked her profusely for pointing this out, whilst at the same time feeling I was an oaf and a numbskull for putting this young woman through this. After she had left, I went into the main office, ripped the calendar up and threw it in the bin. When the detective constables returned, they noticed the calendar had gone from the wall, 'It's gone lads,' I told them. 'The times they are a changing,' I said, quoting Bob Dylan.

Life as a Detective Sergeant at Boscombe was frantic, as always, with about ninety house burglaries a month and dozens of prisoners to wade through every week. I saw less of my family than I should have. Ten-hour days were normal and one could expect two or three 9 am to 10 pm shifts per week, and that's when there were no major incidents to be sucked into.

I had pinned the missing person circulation photograph of Monica Taylor onto my cork notice board in my office which stared down at me each day and said, 'Why haven't you found me? Why are you letting people believe I have committed suicide?' Fate was then to play a hand as it would again later. One morning, I went into the office and went through the daily state for the last twenty-four hours which was my daily routine. The 'daily state' is a computer-generated list of all crimes and prisoners for each police station in the division. It is the detective sergeant's job to allocate prisoners and crimes to the officers coming on duty that morning and, if necessary, to call the 2 pm to 10 pm officers on early to help deal with the daily mayhem. As frequently happened, I ran out of officers, and noticed one local lad had been arrested and was in the cells for burgling a shop during the night. His name was Peter Rabbit who was a well-known local villain whom I had dealt with before. To help the lads out I took the job on myself and drove down to Bournemouth police station, which was also the central lock up. Rabbit had been caught by an alert uniformed officer who stopped and searched him on his way back from a burglary with a bag full of cigarettes; it looked pretty straight forward. Rabbit tried the usual weak routine of an excuse by saying he had 'found the property and was taking it to the police station,' when I reminded him that he was caught walking in the opposite direction. He coughed the job (admitted full responsibility and made a statement under caution) and I got him a coffee, gave him a cigarette, lit my pipe up and we then sat back for a real chat about who was doing what locally.

Peter did not want to go to prison and needed to come up with something pretty good to reduce the term he was likely to get. He knew the ropes as he was one of my registered informants, but like most informants, he only knew what he did because he was bang at it anyway. He told me that a family of villains were operating as house breakers in the Southbourne area of my patch. The gang was led by the father, with his sons and their friends working in the team. Peter knew of a house they intended to burgle as they had already cased it previously and he agreed to point out the house to me. We then talked about local fences – receivers of stolen goods. Thieves don't usually give away their own fences but they will give away other villains' outlets. He told me that there was an old guy, (he meant about fifty) who owned a hotel in Boscombe and who took a lot of stolen property from the older more established Bournemouth villains; he also offered to point out where he lived. That evening we set out in my cool-looking slime green Ford Capri (the Escort had rusted out so badly my driver's seat nearly fell through the floor) for a tour of the patch. Peter pointed out the house in Southbourne which was the intended burglary target.

We then headed into Sea Road. 'There's the place,' and he pointed to none other than the Costa del Sol hotel, while sinking down out of sight in the back seat.

'The old guy in there takes lots of stuff, particularly wine, spirits and cigarettes,' Rabbit said.

I knew that Peter Taylor operated a bar and restaurant within the Costa del Sol complex and these commodities could easily be disposed of under the cover of a legitimate business. Whilst his conviction for dealing in stolen cars was years before, his dishonest nature had not gone away; it all made a lot of sense.

I charged Rabbit with burglary later that day and prepared the court file for his appearance before the Magistrates the following morning. I also contacted Jack Badstock, a young energetic detective sergeant who ran a small surveillance crime squad which fed off this type of hot intelligence. I explained the full circumstances of the planned burglary, guaranteed him that my informant was reliable and left the rest to him.

A day or two later during the afternoon, I was in my office wading through the usual tsunami of crime reports when the phone rang.

'Hi, Notty, it's Jack Badstock; that job you gave us came off, but not where you said. We plotted up on the target address, but they didn't like the look of it for some reason and did one round the corner. They're all bang to rights, but the old boy in charge of them, their father, wants a deal. He says he knows something about Monica Taylor's disappearance; you're dealing with that, aren't you?'

I told him I was and would be with him in warp factor five. I spoke to Jack at the central lock up in Bournemouth. We both knew that a conviction for burglary in a house was an almost certain one-way ticket to jail, persons charged and awaiting trial don't usually stand much of a chance for bail either. Our boss, Detective Chief Superintendent Scott, was a martinet extraordinaire, and if we even thought about giving bail to a housebreaker, our CID careers would come to an almost certain end. I didn't have much slack to play with.

Louis Percival Matthews was fifty-three years of age when I first met him in the cold impersonal interview room adjoining the cells, two floors beneath Bournemouth police station. He looked somewhat like Captain Ahab of *Moby Dick* fame, all beard but no moustache. Louis had a lot of form going back over the years for embezzlement, theft and general acts of villainy. He had a serious countenance and knew the book would be thrown at him; you can't take your sons on a housebreaking spree and expect to get away with it lightly. He was, however, a man of some sort of honour. He was willing to take as much pain away from his sons as he was able and would gladly have done their time for them if he could. Louis was also that very rare creature often referred to but rarely encountered; he was an 'old fashioned villain' and baulked at murder. I was straight with him from the start. I told him I couldn't arrange bail or influence any change in the charges of burglary they all faced. The best I could offer would be to send a letter to the judge through the prosecutor outlining that he had been of great help – if indeed he was to be. Louis did not take much persuading; it was my golden rule never to lie to a villain or promise something I couldn't deliver. It usually took a little longer, that was all.

Louis then unburdened himself of the following; during the mid-1950s, he had been a motor trader and had come into contact with Peter Taylor at his garage in Sea Road. He described how they had bought and sold cars to each other; sometimes the cars were stolen and had been re-plated. In the 1960s, Peter Taylor bought three properties in Sea Road which he was to turn into the Costa del Sol. There were some sitting tenants in the properties and Matthews helped Taylor harass them until they left. They resorted to removing the tenants' furniture, pulling up floor boards in their flats, piling up junk outside the tenants' doors and other nasty tricks. During the 1970s, Matthews saw Taylor on a frequent basis and regularly sold him stolen jewellery and antiques. He painted a picture of a group of older criminals with confidence in each other who mixed legitimate business with criminality. Thus, the information of Rabbit was corroborated by the very person he had supplied information about. In November 1981, Matthews engaged in a transaction with Taylor to dispose of some stolen silver. They did not meet at the Costa del Sol because Peter was worried his wife would report any criminal activity. From enquiries I had made with her friends I had established that Monica was a very lady-like person of high moral integrity. During this meeting, Matthews described how Taylor used to go on and on about his wife and how she was mucking him about financially. Peter Taylor was obsessed that he was going to lose substantially in any divorce proceedings and Matthews said that it seemed to weigh heavily on his mind.

In January 1982, Taylor contacted him again and wanted to discuss some business proposals with him, so they met the following day in a local pub. Taylor said to him, 'She has got to have an accident, she's got to go,' referring to his wife. He said he had the keys to her flat and could get in any time he wished, and initially proposed drugging her milk or hitting her over the head. He suggested her body could be disposed of in the New Forest or by dumping it in the sea or down an old mine shaft in Cornwall. Matthews said that Taylor had got rid of old identifiable car parts down a mine shaft some years before. It seemed however that he did not want to kill her on his own and asked him for help; he offered him £500. Matthews told me that he was not interested in getting involved in murder and rowed backwards as fast as possible. He did however suggest that he may be able to find a hit man in London and a plan was hatched to hire somebody to do the job for £2,000, which is all that could be scraped together. Peter Taylor developed the idea that if someone was to be found he wanted to make it look like a break-in gone wrong or an accident. He in turn would ensure that he had an alibi for the relevant time. Matthews, who was always on the scrounge, wheedled £25 out of Taylor to go to London to find a hit man.

Matthews went on to explain that he made no attempt to look for anybody to kill Monica. He never went to London and never had any intention of doing so. He saw Taylor a few days later and gave him a story that one of the two men he had in mind was in prison and the other was on the run from the police. He said that Taylor was becoming increasingly obsessed with killing Monica and he didn't want to be involved in any way. About three months later, Matthews read about Monica's disappearance in the *Bournemouth Echo,* and was shocked to have been involved even in the preparatory stage. He hoped that Peter hadn't killed her but had a bad feeling in the pit of his stomach. He phoned Taylor a little nervously and found him to be curt, but was invited around to see him at the Costa del Sol. When he met Taylor, he described him as very guarded as he believed his phone was being tapped and he was under surveillance. Matthews told him that he had read about Monica's disappearance and asked him what had happened to her. He replied that she'd upped and gone. Taylor described how the police had questioned him several times and searched his property but added, 'They won't find anything here.'

Matthews explained to me that he continued to see Taylor occasionally, usually in the bar at the Costa del Sol where he frequently got free drinks. Taylor complained that he would have difficulty selling his garage premises as he would have to wait seven years for her to be presumed dead.

When Matthews asked, 'What if she comes back?' Taylor replied, 'She won't, she's gone for good.'

Matthews finished by saying that the last time he saw Taylor was in the bar at the hotel. Taylor was in a bad mood and towards the end of the evening he asked Louis if he felt cold and added, 'I'm sure the bloody bitch is watching me.'

Louis Percival Matthews duly made a full witness statement and promised to give evidence if required. I compiled a full file containing all the witness statements and documents including Monica's affidavit and diaries and submitted it to my senior officers for instructions. I was hoping for some kind of covert operation, or at best the recommendation that we charge Taylor with murder. Not a chance, I was told by my boss; one villain's word against another's is worthless. It was still a potential suicide and since no body had been found, she could still be alive. I was told to re-interview Taylor but not to mention Matthews. I had about as much chance of getting to the truth with him as flying to the sun in a chocolate rocket.

On 29 March 1984, almost exactly two years from the date of Monica's disappearance, DI Geoff Lumbard and I interviewed Peter Taylor again. He started off in his usual amiable manner, the DI engaging him in non-threatening small talk about his wife. He felt that she would not have lasted long on her own and she may have joined the Moonies or some other cult. He threw in that she may have run off with another man but had nothing tangible upon which to base this. He also offered that she may have gone to Ruan Minor in Cornwall as they spent many happy holidays in that area, but again said that she would be unlikely to survive for long on her own. It was put to him that Monica's friends had told us that she was stronger than she had been and he agreed, adding that her language had been less lady-like than in the past.

He told us that a man he vaguely knew had seen a woman answering Monica's description in Lymington about a year before. I asked for this person's name and address and asked why he hadn't told the police. He then made an uncharacteristic slip and said that whilst buying hydrochloric acid from a chemist in Boscombe, he saw a woman who looked very similar to his wife, and he thought the earlier report from the acquaintance had been one of mistaken identity. He was asked to supply this casual acquaintance's name but never did. I asked him why he was buying acid to which he replied that he used it to clean grease from cookers in the apartments by soaking cooker parts in a bath of acid. He was then told that we had been informed that he had been trying to find somebody to kill her. He started to become very irate, denying this and angrily demanding to know who had told us. The mask slipped just that once, and the real dark Peter Taylor glared out, it seemed mainly at me; it was personal. We got no further with him and I told him that this case wasn't closed, nor would it be until we had got to the truth.

Enquiries in Ruan Minor proved negative and checking every old disused tin mine in Cornwall was out of the question. It was in that year that Monica's father died of cancer; I suspect the disappearance of his daughter and the grief which he went through compounded his final agony. The final entry in the missing person's file that year was 'enquiries continue'.

CHAPTER 7

When the Devil Walked in Iford Lane

Monday 28 July 1986 was a day I won't forget. I had been on duty since three that morning, dealing with a serious assault by a man on his girlfriend. I had been questioning and taking written statements from the victim, witnesses and finally the suspect who I charged that afternoon with inflicting grievous bodily harm. His reply after charge was, 'I love her.' Such is the distorted thinking of many a wife beater. I had just worked eight days in a row and lost half a night's sleep, so was looking forward to my day off the next day. I was sitting in the main CID office at Bournemouth central police station, which is near the cell block, finishing off the court papers which were required by the prosecutor for his appearance before the Magistrate's Court the next day. Detective Inspector Penny walked into the office puffing on his pipe and tossed a telex in my direction. Telexes are a thing of the past now, more or less. Before computers were ubiquitous, we relied on these rolls of printed paper, which came from machines in control rooms everywhere with up to date information from other forces.

He said, 'Do you think we ought to have a look at this, Tone?'

DI Penny had been my DS in Weymouth, a serious, sombre thoughtful man but one with a bone-dry sense of humour. I looked quizzically at the faint type-written piece of paper which had come via the control room (where emergency calls are received and actioned) at Winfrith Police HQ. It was a report from a uniformed patrol officer which stated that he had attended a fire at a house in Shelton Road, Southbourne, Bournemouth, which was my patch. The report continued 'Firemen have found the body of a woman in one room and her head in another.'

I replied to DI Penny, 'Yes, Sir, I think we better had.'

Together with a car full of detectives we set off at speed from the central police station arriving ten minutes later outside the house in Southbourne. This is a pleasant suburb with broad tree-lined roads; the only reason this area ever appeared on the police radar was because of the occasional house burglary. Tony Rogers was already there. He was the detective inspector for Winton, Kinson and Boscombe and my direct boss. He told us that he had arranged with our uniform friends to have a cordon placed around the house; entry was limited to certain specialists and a constable was on duty keeping a log of those who entered and left. These would include the doctor (to pronounce that the victim was dead – rather academic, I appreciate), the crime scene examiners, (called scenes of crimes officers in those days) and the Senior Investigating Officer (SIO), usually one of two detective superintendents from HQ. As we waited outside the house for the arrival of these specialists in the pouring rain all trying to shelter under DI Rogers's golfing umbrella, he told us what he knew. A nineteen-year-old youth named Lee Baker had cycled up to a teenage girl, his former girlfriend, whilst she was walking along Boscombe High Street and told her that he had killed her mother and her dog and set the house on fire. He then cycled off in the direction of the main shops. The police radio I was carrying then spluttered into life and a report came through that a young woman had been stabbed in Cecil Road, Boscombe and the offender had run off. Within minutes another report came over the air of a man stabbed in Iford Lane which is about a mile away from where we were. Tony Rogers asked me to go there quickly and find out what was going on. I hurried to my car and took with me one of the detectives at the scene; he also happened to be an experienced officer, but more importantly a muscle-bound fitness fanatic.

We arrived outside a detached house at the Christchurch Road end of Iford Lane and in the driveway we found the dead body of a middle-aged man later identified as Clive Rattue. His chest was soaked in blood and he had left a trail from the house next door. I established that Mr Rattue was returning home from work and had just got off a bus in Christchurch Road, and was walking down a side alley towards his house when he was stabbed. The knife, which was double edged, penetrated his chest and had passed through his heart, exiting at the back. He had also been shot in the back with a crossbow bolt. He then walked to the nearest house, rang the bell, and when he received no answer, walked down the drive to the front door of the next house along the road where he collapsed and died through loss of blood. How he was able to walk the distance he did with such a major injury was something I would not have believed possible, but he did. Mr Rattue was the unluckiest man in the world; he shouldn't have been there. He had been laid off from his job at Fawley Oil refinery in Southampton the week before but had negotiated an extra week. This was that week.

My detective partner and I made urgent, if not frantic, house to house enquiries, desperately looking for witnesses. Was this linked to the house fire in Shelton Road and decapitation of the woman there? Was there a link to the other stabbing in Cecil Road? Whilst we were looking for witnesses, another report came over the radio of a German language student who had been shot by a man with a crossbow further down Iford Lane, but he had managed to run off before the assailant closed with him. After our attempts to find witnesses or gather any clue as to why this mayhem was happening around us we set out to track down and inform Mr Rattue's family of this tragedy. He was closely related to Peter Rabbit who was my informant in the Taylor case and I had met Mr Rattue occasionally when chasing Peter for one misdemeanour or another. His wife was at home and devastated by the news. It is a most awful experience for anyone to say goodbye in the morning to one's closest friend as they set out routinely for work and are then informed that they will never see them alive again. Breaking this kind of news to people is one of the worst duties a police officer has to do, and despite all attempts at remaining professional, grief is infectious. Once that was done and a policewoman in the role of family liaison officer installed in the house, we set off for a local pub to find his sons. Needless to say, they too were devastated by the loss of their father and completely broke down. This sad duty accomplished, we joined the search for the killer which was only just getting started.

Police officers were drafted into Bournemouth from all over the county and the Hampshire Police were on standby to assist if needed. It was established that the lady in Shelton Road had been stabbed twice, before her head was cut off. The head was placed on a pillow in a bedroom and the body was found in an adjoining bedroom. The dog had been shot with a crossbow. Mr Rattue had been shot with a crossbow and stabbed to death with a double-edged knife. The young woman in Cecil Road had also been stabbed with a double-edged knife and was a friend of Baker's ex-girlfriend. She suffered a single deep wound which by sheer chance missed all her vital organs and she thankfully made a full recovery. A puncture wound from a knife will show the edge of the blade in a sharp V shape and usually the opposite edge as a blunt straight cut. These wounds were V shaped on both edges of the incision; it had to be a dagger. The German student had been shot with a crossbow and also survived. With the use of a double-edged knife (later found to be a Fairbairn-Sykes commando fighting knife), and crossbow in these attacks as well as the admission that Baker had made to his former girlfriend, it was clear all these crimes were linked.

Bournemouth was swamped with police that evening and night; just about every officer who could walk was deployed. There was great fear of further killings. I remained with my muscle-bound fitness fanatic partner and requisitioned the services of Mark, another of my detective constables who just happened to be six feet six inches tall and also played a mean game of rugby. He had a jaw squarer than Desperate Dan and could be relied upon in a tight spot. I have always been able to choose men wisely. Every pub, club, alley and street in Bournemouth and Poole were checked and rechecked. All of Baker's associates, friends, family and haunts were visited, all to no avail. Mercifully no further killings took place. By three am I was exhausted and finished duty with instructions to be on duty again at eight am that morning. Tony Rogers somehow had the stamina to stay on and worked right through the night, setting up the Home Office Large Major

Enquiry System, which is established for all major crime investigations, and is also known as HOLMES.

The next morning continued in the same frantic way. We were just in the process of completing briefings of the various teams of police officers when news arrived that a single patrolling uniformed officer had arrested Baker. The officer was attending a routine report of theft at a housing estate about a mile and a half away from the crime scene in Iford Lane, when Baker appeared out of the bushes and surrendered himself to the officer without any trouble. The uniformed officer was fully aware of the events of the previous day and managed to retain his composure and calmly talked to the suspect until reinforcements arrived. Baker was then taken to the central lock up in Bournemouth.

I was given the task of seeing him in his cell and obtaining his consent to be examined by a doctor and our crime scene examiners. It is important in serious cases involving violence to note marks, scars and abrasions on a prisoner's body as soon after arrest as possible, as this may have a bearing on the crime they are suspected of. For example, if a person claims self-defence and has a number of recent injuries, then those are material and could well influence what, if any charge, he should face. It is important that the court and in particular the prosecution and defence lawyers have as much information as you can gather. It is the job of a police investigator to gather all the evidence, not just that useful to the prosecution. When I walked into his cell he stood up and towered over me being much taller, and I suspect, much fitter than me. My hair immediately stood on end and I must confess to feeling I was in the presence of a very evil person. He was polite and content to be examined. I asked him if he had killed more than one person or did we have more than one killer on the loose? He said, 'No,' and that he had done them all!

DI Tony Rogers and I were then given the task of interviewing – police terminology for questioning – him. In 1986 the police nationally had and were going through a number of serious miscarriage of justice trials which had led to a substantial loss of confidence in the police. As a result of this, the government planned to radically alter and codify the way police dealt with suspects. Until the mid-1980s, police interviews comprised police officers questioning a suspect and recording afterwards what was said in their pocket books to the best of their recollection. Needless to say, on many occasions when the case got to court, the recollection of what the police said they said, differed from what the accused said they said. With the decline of confidence in the police, more and more people, particularly jurors, believed the accused. I for one couldn't wait for the change-over to tape recorded interviews, but while the interview rooms were being refurbished, the technology installed, and the laws passed, we used a stop-gap measure. This was to write the questions and answers laboriously onto a sheet of paper as they occurred during the questioning. This badly reduced the flow of an interview, but it was the law, so we just had to get on with it.

During the course of the day we interviewed Baker several times. He showed no emotion or remorse at having killed two people, and readily admitted what he had done. He was quite content to admit killing his former girlfriend's mother, having stabbed her twice; the second time to make sure she was dead, he quietly told us. Tony Rogers asked him how he had cut off her head and why, but he didn't want to say. He also told him that he had been labelled a 'Rambo killer' by the *Sun* newspaper which seemed to amuse him for a time. I asked why he had killed Mr Rattue but he could not explain that either. He remembered it well enough, describing how he had shot him in the back with the crossbow and then walked up to him. Mr Rattue turned around and said, 'What did you do that for?' at which he stabbed him in the chest and walked off. He didn't stop to look at what he had done; he just walked away, almost unconcerned. He told us that he was responsible for shooting his crossbow at another person in Iford Lane (the German student) and fully admitted stabbing a young woman in Cecil Road, Boscombe as she answered her door to him. She was an acquaintance of his former girlfriend. Again, he stabbed her, turned and walked away, not looking back. He wanted to punish his former girlfriend by these murderous assaults on her mother and friend. He then quite unexpectedly said that he wanted to go out in a blaze of glory. He planned to go to the petrol filling station at the top of Pokesdown Hill, Boscombe, and jam open the petrol pumps so the fuel would run down the hill, then set the whole scene on fire. He would have killed the garage attendant if necessary. The possible chaos and deaths that could have ensued would have been horrific. However, the opportunity never presented itself because the whole area was awash with police and he abandoned his plan. Throughout the time I spent with him he was calm and emotionless; it was as if he had just stepped on a couple of insects, not taken the lives of two decent people and tried to kill two more. At the end of the last interview that day, being about 6 pm, Tony Rogers' head fell onto the interview room table in sheer exhaustion; he had worked over thirty-two hours non-stop.

Lee Baker had experienced a difficult life. His mother couldn't cope with all her children, most of whom, including Lee, were taken into care. His father took little interest in him and he was not happy at a boarding school to which he was sent. In fact, sketches were found at his accommodation by police which illustrated death and destruction being visited upon the school and its teachers. He was a gifted artist and drew very professional looking pictures on a 'Conan the Barbarian' theme except that the violence depicted was pretty graphic. He had been referred for psychotherapy treatment when younger to treat his depression and anger problems, but he never followed it up. Baker was seen by psychiatrists before his court appearance at Winchester Crown Court, who considered that he was not insane in accordance with the McNaughton rules – in other words, that he had not proved to be 'labouring under a defect of reason'; he knew 'the nature and quality of the act he was committing' and knew it was wrong – and was considered 'sane' and fit to stand trial.

The police traced a number of Baker's friends, one of whom knew a former girlfriend of his. He told us that Baker had attacked her after she had expressed a wish to be free of him. The person explained that Baker had wanted to control and manipulate people, and if he didn't get his way, he became violent. Clearly his murderous behaviour was a drastic extension of this same pattern of behaviour. So, if Baker had been deemed sane and fit to stand trial, was he bad or evil? Had he undergone psychotherapy treatment and further investigations into his mental state and behavioural issues, could he have received treatment to address the problems he clearly had? As a police officer of over thirty years' service I have never failed to be disappointed at the lack of investment in the care of those affected by mental illness. Our scientists seem to be able to peer into the far corners of the universe but are unable to peer with such confidence into the human brain.

Baker appeared at Winchester Crown Court in June 1987 and after a two-week trial which centred on his mental state, he was convicted of two counts of murder, one of attempted murder, arson and assault. He was sentenced to life imprisonment. A uniformed control room inspector as well as the policemen and women on duty on 28 and 29 July 1986 saved the lives of a lot of people in Bournemouth that night.

CHAPTER 8

The Reckoning:
The Case of Peter Taylor Part Three

In 1988, as a result of some unseen intervention by the goddess Fortuna, I was promoted to the rank of inspector. I was posted to Christchurch where I was a uniform shift inspector for Christchurch, Wimborne and Ferndown, areas not known for much in the way of crime. I worked a straight eight hours and was relieved promptly by the inspector whose shift always followed mine. I always felt guilty at so little to report and was tempted to elaborate, but lacked the creative flair needed. I used to go home swearing blind that there must be a shed-load of work I was not doing but I'm blessed if I knew what it was. The biggest excitement I had, in the seven months I was a uniformed inspector, was when four beefy louts decided to mix it with the one and only uniformed constable on the beat in Christchurch High Street. I answered the call for assistance with Woman Police Sergeant Lyn Hart and the three of us fought toe to toe with the hooligans. Two ran off, and the remaining two we captured and shackled together with both our handcuffs. They looked an odd sight when the police van eventually arrived to cart them off to the cells as they were handcuffed back to back because they would not stop fighting. Getting them into the police van really was quite a challenge, but I didn't want to risk taking their handcuffs off because they really were both quite muscular. I had been a bit of a male chauvinist in the past, but I must say there are some women in the Dorset Police I would rather have had at my side than some men I have worked with. Lyn fought like a tigress and showed herself to be like many of her female colleagues to be made of steel. She later rose through the ranks to become a chief superintendent; the system does get it right sometimes.

One night in the autumn of that year, I was on patrol with Norman, a uniformed constable in a panda car around

Christchurch. Norman was a member of the Salvation Army and a blunt gruff spoken Scot. A sea fog had rolled in across the coast reducing visibility drastically and making everything look distorted and eerie in the gloom. As we approached a roundabout on the bypass, I saw an unusual shape near a tree which made up the centre of the roundabout.

'That's a car there,' I said.

Norman thought otherwise. 'No, Sir, it's the bushes.'

'Stop a minute; let's take a look,' I said.

It was very still, about four in the morning and the fog made it seem almost deathly quiet. We walked from the police car onto the roundabout which had an abundance of shrubbery and several trees. There in the dank cold we found the tangled remains of a car which had smashed into a mature tree and broken off the bark at the point of impact. The car had broken into three pieces and must have been travelling at high speed. Outside what was left of the driver's compartment and lying motionless on his back, was a young man. He was cold and dead. He had no injuries that could be seen and had died of massive internal trauma. We searched the immediate vicinity for other injured people but found none. I called in the few officers we had and together we made a more extensive search in case someone had crawled away to die literally in a ditch; it has happened. We found no one, and after the area was swept by a sharp-nosed police dog, I was satisfied we had not missed anyone. The vehicle registration number was checked and it was found that the car had been reported stolen from Southampton, a city twenty-five miles to the east. Obviously, the car thief was enjoying a fast burn up along what he thought was a dual carriageway, not a bypass punctuated by a roundabout, which he saw too late appearing out of the fog. I dealt with the whole incident in a mechanical, almost robotic way. I arranged for the specialist traffic officers to investigate and report the crash, the next of kin were informed and all evidential considerations taken care of. I even accompanied the body to the mortuary to comply with strict evidential rules. Not until I got home did it occur to me that I had been dealing with the death of a human being. A petty thief maybe; but deserving of more thought and care than just removing a piece of scrap metal from the highway. He was some mother's son and his loss would be badly felt in his community. He was only a kid. I had become too hard, dealing with death so frequently; it was time to take stock and remember I was a human and not a machine. I kept this to the forefront of my mind after that.

My escape from CID did not last long, much to my wife's disappointment and I was soon back in the 'CID family' working as the DI for Boscombe, Winton and Kinson, all part of Bournemouth, and interesting parts at that. On a Sunday afternoon in November 1991, I was working in my office at Winton catching up on paperwork. I was weekend cover for the Bournemouth Division, and my opposite number, DI Chubb, was on a rest day.

The phone rang and the conversation went something like this, 'Hello mate, is Chris Chubb there?'

I explained that he was weekend off and asked if I could help. The caller, a gruff spoken man, said that he knew Mr Chubb personally and only wanted to speak to him. I asked him for a brief idea of what he wanted to see him about.

He said, 'It's about a bloke called Peter Taylor.'

I sat bolt upright and said, 'I know Peter Taylor I investigated the disappearance of his wife Monica.'

He said 'Lovely lady, lovely lady, too good for him. It's about something similar; he wants somebody done like.'

I established that nothing was going to happen within the next twenty-four hours and obtained all the necessary contact details. I then spoke to Chris and passed him all the information, and he went to see this person the very next day. It seemed that the word was out that Peter Taylor wanted somebody else murdered; this time it was his son-in-law who was in the process of an acrimonious divorce with one of his daughters.

Fortunately for me (yet again) Chris Chubb was an outstanding highly experienced former Regional Crime Squad officer and to put a cherry on the top of the cake, the detective superintendent was John (Jake) Homer, one of the most dynamic and accomplished detectives in the force. Between them they put together a full-scale undercover operation, I was glad to be the tea boy and typing checker in the background. An undercover officer was inserted into the equation and monitored by a specialist police team over a period of weeks as he negotiated with Peter Taylor about the killing of his son in law. The sum for the job was to be £15,000 for which the undercover officer would receive £2,000 in advance. Photographs of the intended victim were passed by Taylor to the would-be hit man. These were cuttings from a local paper of the intended victim holding up a fish he had caught in a local competition. It was not the only fish being caught; a bigger game unbeknown to Taylor was afoot!

He made one oblique reference to Monica when he said to the undercover officer 'I'd do it myself; wouldn't be the first time in this house, but the law has got a long memory.'

These were crucial words, but just one sentence. What he didn't know was that all this conversation was being covertly tape recorded. I am being deliberately vague about the precise mechanics of how all this was done, but I am sure that it will be understood that these tactics must remain secret.

Taylor wanted his son-in-law killed because his daughter had been engaged in a messy divorce. There had been problems with her marriage and acrimony on both sides. It is not my wish to go into those details any further as it would unnecessarily uncover old wounds. The point was that she wanted a divorce but was concerned about losing her house and grounds. It can be clearly seen where this is all leading, as it starts to mirror the financial strain Taylor was under during his divorce proceedings with Monica. Most fathers would probably have counselled their daughters along the lines of having to accept some financial loss, but with a good case against the husband for inappropriate conduct and a good lawyer the impact could be minimised. But not Peter Taylor; no, the course he recommended was to murder the husband and grab all the money – not the average advice a father would give to his daughter.

During the course of conversations with the undercover officer, Taylor made certain suggestions. He proposed the murder be made to look like a robbery or an accident, and he wanted to know the precise time so that he could construct a rock-solid alibi. He put considerable thought and deviousness into his plans.

However, after each covert operation, John Homer, Chris Chubb and myself sat and read the transcripts of the undercover officer's conversations with Taylor. One thing struck me was that whilst Taylor was making it clear that he wanted the victim 'taking out', or 'finishing off,' he never ever used the word 'kill,' There was even less evidence against his daughter. We needed the 'kill' word in the evidence or a smart barrister would exploit this flaw and suggest Taylor just wanted the victim 'roughing up.' The undercover officer had agreed with Taylor that he would carry out the hit on Friday 29 November 1991 as the husband left home in the morning to walk his dog. It was agreed between them that his daughter would telephone a nearby public telephone box when her husband left their house to forewarn the hit man. Chris and Jake constructed the sequence including a surprise that they had woven into the arrangements.

On the Friday morning at 0745 am the daughter made the agreed call to the telephone box as she had been told to by her father. When the call was answered she asked the recipient for his name, which was a prearranged code name. Being satisfied she was talking to the would-be assassin, she told him that her husband had left the farm to walk their dog. She described what he was wearing and confirmed the direction he had taken.

The supposed hit man asked her, 'Are you sure you want him killed?'

She was taken aback, paused and said, 'Yes.'

He asked her again. 'Are you sure you want him killed?'

She again replied, 'Yes.'

Within minutes the front door bell of her substantial property sounded, she answered it to find the Regional Crime Squad had come calling, and she was arrested for conspiracy to commit murder. Almost simultaneously Peter Taylor stepped from the sunken bath in his sumptuous detached house on the cliff tops at Bournemouth to be arrested for solicitation and conspiracy to commit murder.

Now it was my turn; this time I wasn't grappling around without evidence. All his conversations had been taped, all these conversations transcribed, and I had the whole operation, chapter and verse to put to him. Detective Sergeant Tony Cox, a gentlemanly career detective, was my partner. Over the next couple of days, we carried out formal interviews with Peter Taylor and his daughter in the interview rooms in the detention block at Bournemouth in the presence of their solicitors. I made sure as always that I was immaculately dressed in my favourite (lucky) blue pin stripe suit and blue tie. The interview room is sombre, plain and has painted tile walls. There is not much to look at other than the person sitting opposite, in his case me, and Tony Cox. We both had to look impeccable and maintain a psychological edge. The first interview with Taylor was an open question introduction to the case in which I revealed nothing of the police operation, but wanted to establish certain facts, such as his relationship with his daughter and son-in-law and his general background. He was his usual charming, smiling, suave self. He said absolutely nothing throughout, not even 'no comment' which is the standard reply from professional criminals; he just sat there mute. I had grown a full set beard since my last meeting with him seven years before and lost a bit of weight as I was into a fitness regime in my middle-age.

After the formal interview had been concluded and while I was packing up and labelling the interview tapes and collecting my papers, Taylor spoke the only words he would ever say to me. 'Haven't we met before?'

I opened my file of papers to the back cover on which I had sellotaped Monica's photograph, which I had taken down from my notice board. I slid the file and photograph across the interview room table and said, 'I investigated the disappearance of Monica.'

His face went like thunder; the mask slipped; the real Peter Taylor glared out. The air in the interview room was charged with electricity; you could almost touch it.

In the next interview, I began revealing the police case, the photograph of the intended victim holding the fish; the admission that he would 'do it himself, wouldn't be the first time in this house.' I played the tape recordings of his suggestions of how to cover the killing by making it look like a robbery gone wrong. I deliberately left a long pause after each disclosure and could feel him wince. Each revelation impacted like an Exocet missile hitting a stricken ship. He visibly went lower and lower, and I must confess to a grim satisfaction in watching him. He had murdered his wife of 27 years and the mother of three children for money and no other reason; and was preparing to kill another man for the same. I bore him little pity.

Peter Taylor and his daughter were both charged with conspiracy to commit murder and remanded to appear at Winchester Crown Court where they eventually pleaded guilty to this offence. The decision as to whether to charge Peter Taylor with the murder of Monica however; was a far more difficult one. The only additional evidence we had since Louis Matthew's statement was the one sentence, 'I'd do it myself, wouldn't be the first time in this house.' It was imperative therefore that the evidence which had been gathered in the undercover operation and used to prove the conspiracy to murder, could also be used to support a murder which had occurred nine years earlier. Unfortunately, I could bet my pension that the defence would try to sever the indictment of conspiracy to commit murder from any charge of murder of Monica on the grounds that it was a different offence, to which he had pleaded guilty and any mention of it would prejudice the jury. It was very difficult during the 1970s and '80s to admit this kind of evidence and time and again juries acquitted people because they were not told all the facts about the defendant's criminal behaviour: – this is one reason why so many people suspected of child abuse during that period were not prosecuted.

Once again fortune was on my side, as the Branch Crown Prosecutor was a highly experienced lawyer, John Revell, and he was able to entice one of the best barristers on the western circuit to take the case, John Aspinall QC. They agreed that if we could use the evidence in the conspiracy to commit murder charge, then we would have a fair chance of convicting Taylor of murdering his wife years before. John

Revell bravely decided to approve the charging of Taylor with the murder of Monica. While I was delighted, I knew how thin our case was. But for the ability of these two talented lawyers and the advocacy skills in particular of Mr Aspinall, a born wordsmith, I doubt we would have ever charged Taylor with the murder. Mr Aspinall was able to lace together the case of conspiracy to murder the son-in-law with the murder of Monica by highlighting facts from each case which were strikingly similar. These were as follows: divorce proceedings were in action in both cases; both spouses stood to gain good financial settlements thus reducing the assets of the other parties; Louis Matthews was approached to either kill Monica or find somebody that would, the undercover officer being solicited for the same reason; both the murder of Monica and intended murder of the son-in-law were to look like a crime gone wrong or an accident; the hit man was to be paid for doing the job, Matthews having the offer of money, the undercover officer receiving a down payment with more to come.

The trial judge accepted this argument and allowed the inclusion of this similar fact evidence in the trial of Taylor for the murder of his wife; so the jury had before them all the facts, to the chagrin of the defence. Armed with this argument and making the most of Taylor's use of hydrochloric acid to dispose of Monica's remains, (which he had said he had used to clean grease from cookers), Mr Aspinall presented a case so convincing that it took the jury just over two hours to return a unanimous verdict of guilty to murder. It was Friday 19 March 1993, two weeks short of ten years since Monica went missing. I remember driving home in the car that night. There was a sense of elation with the team of officers who had made this result possible; it had been a long, hard slog. However, despite the success, I could not help feeling a great sadness; Monica had died a lonely and dreadful death at the hands of her husband of many years, and there was nowhere to lay a flower on her grave. I got the distinct sense that Monica was pleased that the record had been set straight and that she hadn't committed suicide. But there was a feeling of sadness that her husband was starting a long prison sentence in his mid-sixties, and Monica's father had died not knowing what had happened to her. There were no winners really. I didn't go to the usual celebratory drink at the end of the trial. When you've been eyeball to eyeball with a killer and got to know the victim as well as your sister, it just doesn't feel right. I did often celebrate successful operations with colleagues and have put plenty of pound notes across the bar for the first round, but as I said, some cases were just too personal.

CHAPTER 9

Ethical Dilemmas

Doctor Allen Anscombe is a highly qualified Home Office forensic pathologist, part of whose responsibilities were to undertake forensic autopsies in the whole of Dorset and elsewhere when required. I got to work with Doctor Anscombe many times over the years and found him to be quiet, deeply thoughtful and a complete gentleman. The first autopsy I attended as a young detective sergeant was an utterly horrible experience; to witness the dicing and slicing of the human body is for me not particularly pleasant, the smell and sight of a corpse with all vital organs including the brain removed is quite ghastly. I almost passed out the first time I attended one. I had been assigned a case of suicide to investigate, and I was also there to ensure that death was not due to an accident, or even a murder being made to look like suicide. Allen and the Crime Scene examiners appeared completely absorbed in their work as the corpse was dissected and samples taken. I was feeling bad to start with, then as the chest was opened up, with what I can only describe as a large set of shears, everything suddenly went white and far away just as it does before you switch off and faint. I somehow just about managed to stay upright and tottered off giving a vague excuse of having to make a phone call. I thought I was going to be violently sick and my mouth filled with saliva but was saved by the fresh air as I staggered outside the mortuary. After a while my green face returned to a whiter shade of pale and I got back just in time for the end of the examination. Had I fainted, I would never have been able to hold my head up high in a CID office ever again. Policemen by their very nature are mickey takers, a detective sergeant with a tendency to pass out at the sight of blood may well have attracted quite a lot of ribbing! As time wore on, I got used to these procedures, but never quite had the enthusiasm that some pathologists I met seemed to exude.

In the late 1980s, when I was working as a detective inspector in Bournemouth, I got a call in my office from one of our scenes of crime officers. He told me that Doctor Anscombe was in the middle of conducting an autopsy and he wanted me to attend the mortuary. It had started out as a routine examination not involving the police, but he felt in this case that H.M. Coroner (to whom he reported) would want an investigation. I drove from central Bournemouth to the mortuary which is situated just off Kings Park in Boscombe. The building has the appearance of an Edwardian bungalow and had the odd name of Rose Cottage. When I got there, Doctor Anscombe had a troubled look on his face; he was right to be concerned. He explained that the deceased was a man in his early eighties who had died as a result of an overdose of paracetamol and morphine, the latter having been administered by the family doctor. The deceased, who I will call Mr Hine, had in the past suffered from testicular cancer and was at the time of his death suffering from bone cancer. Doctor Anscombe considered the dose of morphine to have been on the high side. He further said that the bone cancer he was suffering from was treatable. He also believed that a note had been left on the bedside in which Mr Hine stated that he had taken an overdose and did not want to be resuscitated. Doctor Anscombe showed me into the examination room where the body of Mr Hine lay on a stainless-steel table. I was shown the liver and could see clearly a starburst of ruptures all over this large organ, sure sign of the damage caused by an overdose of paracetamol. Doctor Anscombe told me that despite the fact that these are every day pain killers, they must only be taken in accordance with the instructions and are quite lethal if taken in excess.

There were a number of points to consider. How long after a substantial number of paracetamol tablets have been ingested, can medical intervention be taken and the drugs removed from the stomach? How long do they take to dissolve into the blood system? What medical intervention was possible, legally and practically, and why did the family doctor administer such a high dose of morphine to somebody who was unconscious?

I called on Mrs Hine to investigate further. She was an extremely dignified elderly lady who had been through a terrible ordeal. She described how several days before, she had left her husband in bed in order to do some shopping. He was feeling unwell and had been deteriorating for some time. She was fully aware of his cancer and had accompanied him on numerous occasions to the hospital when he received treatment. When she returned from her shopping trip, her husband was asleep in bed with a note beside him. He had written that he felt having survived the testicular cancer, a further cancer had returned to kill him. He did not want to be a burden on his family, so had taken a large number of paracetamol tablets (over thirty, I recall). He wanted no medical intervention and instructed he be allowed to die. This kind of instruction was relatively uncommon at the time and known as a 'living will.' It was subject of much debate within the medical and legal community, and like a lot of things had started in America some years earlier. It can be argued that to treat a patient who has declined treatment can amount to an assault. The family described Mr Hine as being very 'old fashioned', reminiscent of a Victorian gentleman. He was a marvellous husband and father, but his word was taken as the law; consequently Mrs. Hine respected and obeyed her husband's wishes. She told me that despite having taken such an overdose he did not die immediately. As the evening drew on, she got into bed with her dying husband and lay awake in a desperate and confused state before she eventually fell asleep. When she awoke in the morning, he was still alive. Being at her wits' end, she called a doctor who duly arrived. He was a young man at the beginning of his career. He read the note and considered that due to the lapse of time in taking the paracetamol, the patient's liver would be irreparably damaged. There was no treatment available and taking account of the wishes of Mr Hine, there was nothing further that could be done. The torment of Mrs Hine was unimaginable. Mr Hine remained in a coma until that evening when a second doctor was called and repeated the same opinion as the first. Once again Mrs. Hine went to bed with her husband who survived through the second night. She again called a doctor who this time administered to the patient a hefty dose of morphine. Mr Hine died later that day and the concern was raised by Doctor Anscombe at the routine autopsy, which is where I came in.

Detectives usually deal with bad people who do bad things. Whilst it's not always good guys and bad guys (sometimes it's bad guys and even worse guys) this was a case of very good guys (or at least one) who may have done a bad thing, or not! Mr Hine was going to die, his liver would never have recovered from the damage of thirty plus paracetamol tablets, and he wanted no medical intervention; it was just a matter of time. Should medical intervention have been attempted despite the patient's wishes? Was the injection of morphine mercy killing? If it was, it was only shortening the inevitable; but even so is it still an intentional killing? Murder must have malice aforethought incorporated into the act but manslaughter could apply. I did not relish the thought of putting a doctor in prison; a man to all intents and purposes who had devoted his life to saving life and alleviating suffering. When a detective is faced with ethical difficulties like this there is only one thing to do. Put your hand into the hand of truth and let it lead you where it will. Very fortunately for the detective it is for others to make the prosecutorial decisions based on the law and what is in the public interest.

I interviewed all three doctors who confirmed their action as had been described to me. Doctor number three believed that the patient, while in a coma, was experiencing suffering and pain and gave the injection to alleviate any pain he could be going through. I made a considerable number of enquiries regarding the possibility of patients in comas suffering pain with health professionals. I discovered that there was a body of evidence for this view and obtained statements from a medical doctor and police surgeon to state this in professional terms. I had already been in close liaison with the Crown Prosecution Service (CPS) who considered that no criminal offences had been committed. The family were all relieved with this decision as they had supported the action of their family doctors. The Coroner had no criticism to make of any of the medical practitioners, or of the police investigation and the inquest jury returned a verdict of suicide to the satisfaction of the family. Living wills or instructions to medical professionals – 'Do not attempt resuscitation' (DNAR) – are now relatively common place, but they weren't at the time. The investigator must also be alert for twisted personalities such as Doctor Shipman and Nurse Beverley Allitt – medical professionals who became serial killers. The type of moral issues faced in this case remains one which challenges medical professionals, coroners, police, lawyers, legislators and indeed the public to this day.

Some years later, when I was an operational detective superintendent, I dealt with another case which involved a group of care workers who could have been criminally reckless, bullies; or who killed a patient in their care completely by accident. Late one summer afternoon, I received a telephone call while I was in my office at police headquarters, from Alan Swanton, one of my old Weymouth CID colleagues. He had attended a psychiatric hospital ward where one of the patients had been suffocated during restraint procedures, carried out by nurses and carers in the unit. I told him I would be there immediately, I let my boss know where I was going and drove at some speed to the unit, arriving half an hour later.

The hospital unit, on the outskirts of Bournemouth, was small, cared for about thirty patients, was a modern building and appeared well equipped. Swannie met me at the front and outlined to me the enquiries that he and three other detectives had carried out. The deceased, a man in his forties, had been taken away by paramedics to the accident and emergency department at Poole hospital, but had died on arrival. He had a long history of violent behaviour due to his psychological condition and had inflicted substantial injuries to nurses at the unit in the past, up to and including breaking limbs. One incident involved pushing a nurse down the stairs causing her to be off work for over two months. He was also suspected of not taking his medication.

Swannie explained that the patient had become loud, excitable and aggressive that afternoon which exploded when he took a shoe off and hit a fellow patient with it. Two care assistants caught up with him on the lawn and attempted to encourage him to return to his room and, most importantly, take his medication. He was adamant he would not, broke free of the carers and ran across the lawn. He was stopped by a third carer and as he tried to restrain the patient, they both fell to the floor. The other two carers then caught up and tried to restrain the patient on the lawn. One carer took one arm, a second carer took the other arm, and the third carer, a heavily built man, knelt by the patient's head – he was face down – and gripped both arms. The patient thrashed about; the more he was restrained, the more violent he became and he tried to bite the male carer's legs. This patient had a history of biting his nurses and carers. In order to stop these actions, the carer gripped the patient's head with his knees which had the effect of keeping him face down. The patient then went limp and his whole body relaxed; he had suffocated and despite frantic attempts to revive him, he died. I saw the three carers huddled together in the garden of the unit, they were all completely shaken. Was this manslaughter by gross negligence or was this a tragic accident?

While we would have been completely within the law to arrest all three, I decided to move more slowly and deliberately. We needed to make extensive enquiries at the unit; we needed to get statements from all the witnesses to this tragedy. It had happened on a sunny day in full view of at least a dozen people, and we needed some background on the unit and staff. It being so late, I did not think we would be in a position to question those involved until much later that day, or more likely in the morning. I decided against locking up three carers for the night and advised them to immediately see a solicitor. I wanted them to be able to tell a lawyer everything that had happened and attend Bournemouth police station the following day with their legal representative. Most solicitors in Bournemouth are highly professional competent men and women. One or two are not and will do everything in their power to get their clients off the hook – even when they know they are guilty. Fortunately, the three carers were directed to the office of one of the best criminal law solicitors in Bournemouth, who represented them.

I was able to call more detectives to the scene and very shortly every office and room in the psychiatric unit had been taken over to obtain witness statements of the incident. I personally called into the intelligence cell and ascertained that there had been no incidents of assault, allegations of abuse or any other suspicions in relation to the management and care at the unit. This took all evening.

The next morning the three carers attended the police station with their solicitor. They most certainly had a look of deep dread and were quite frightened about the outcome. One was prepared to be locked up that night and was in possession of an overnight bag. They all provided full accounts of their actions which were corroborated by a number of witnesses who saw the whole thing happen. The three carers freely admitted they had held the patient down on a spongy lawn which had quite long grass. The male carer described how the patient had thrashed about and tried to bite him and he was fearful that if he failed to restrain him, he would break loose and cause injury to another nurse or patient. When the patient became limp it struck them that they may have stifled him and the actions of restraint and force transformed into one of frantic attempts at lifesaving – all to no avail.

I went back with Swannie that morning to re-examine the scene. The lawn had thick, well-maintained grass, which was long, dense and spongy. I could clearly see that if a person's face were pressed against this surface, then suffocation would be the likely result. I next saw the mother of the deceased. She was an elderly woman who loved her son dearly and dutifully visited him regularly at the unit. She knew of his violent behaviour and believed that his psychiatric condition had been caused during a difficult birth – he was a forceps delivery. She was not at all happy at how her son had been restrained.

My personal assessment was that these three carers had acted in what they thought was the best interest of the patient, the other patients and the staff. They had attempted to prevent anyone from getting injured and there was certainly no malice in their actions. I did not want to see them being prosecuted, but again, fortunately, that was not my decision. I had been in contact with the coroner, as it is his duty to investigate all deaths in his area, with the police acting as his agents, which I was. The coroner was of the same opinion as I was and set things in motion for a full inquest.

After collection of all the evidence the Crown Prosecution Service decided there was no criminal liability to be borne by anyone. And again, the coroner made no criticism of those involved and the jury returned a verdict of misadventure. Good training is essential for people who may be called upon to use restraint when all else fails. One problem, however, is that the more a person is restrained, the more likely it is that they will in turn lose all control and reason and find super human energy to overstrain themselves and induce trauma. Most important of all, is clear policy and guidelines from management of institutions as to if and when this tactic should be employed and indeed how.

The NHS in Dorset train all their staff who work in psychiatric units in the prevention and management of violence and aggression (PMVA training). This specialist instruction, which is essential around physically controlling patients who present challenging behaviour which could lead to harming themselves or others, extends over five days of intensive exercises. It emphasises soft restraint and causing the minimum harm to the patient whilst trying to ensure maximum safety to its own staff. Conflict management, pacification of the violently disturbed and a confident, non-aggressive approach are fundamental. Numerous deaths of this type occurred during my police service and continue to happen. The investigation of such deaths and the outcomes continue to remain challenging.

I have dealt with several cases involving death where there has been an absence of malice and/or intent. Once that is established, the investigator must consider: recklessness and whether that arises from gross negligence, which is criminal conduct; incompetence, if so, why; and or an accident. Various parties, including relatives and pressure groups, will be trying to influence investigators this way and that, but the investigator must be led by the truth and the law, which is why close cooperation with the CPS is essential. It is very satisfying for the detective to establish the truth; the fact that at times it does not lead to a prosecution or clears a person of blame is as satisfying as banging up someone who deserves it. The issues surrounding assisted suicide, advances in medical science to maintain life, and the wishes of the terminally ill remain the source of complex ethical dilemmas.

CHAPTER 10

Hunting Wild Boar

The May Day bank holiday weekend of 1990 in Bournemouth, as in most seaside towns, heralded the real start of another holiday season. The pedalos and deck chairs were brought out from winter storage and arranged on the beaches. Ice cream parlours were spruced up and made ready, and slot machines oiled and polished for the influx of happy holiday makers escaping from their desks and factories. The coming weekend promised to be a little different. Association Football Club Bournemouth were at the bottom of the second division and needed to win their last match of the season to stay up. Their opponents, Leeds United, had been relegated from the First Division – no Premier League then – the year before and needed to win this match to be promoted back into the First Division. This in itself should not bode too badly until you put things into context. By 1990 English football hooligans had worked assiduously for twenty years to become the scourge of Europe and the wider world. They were feared wherever they went, and their behaviour had been so bad that some football grounds resembled large zoos with high wire cages around the fans, so everybody was treated like thugs instead of just the few who were. Unfortunately, more than a few visited Bournemouth that May weekend. Leeds United were a well-supported team with fans from all over the country. They also attracted a following of out-and-out thugs such as 'The Service Crew' who carried box cutters or razor knives and attacked opposing fans with ruthless impunity. They frequently had their gang name tattooed boldly on the front of their neck just above the collar line.

Having identified the hooliganism problem, it should also be remembered that a year before, in April 1989, the worst disaster in English football history occurred at Hillsborough stadium in Sheffield. This was an FA cup semi-final match between Liverpool and Nottingham Forest, two of the best teams in English football. It was a very important match which had attracted a crowd of over fifty thousand people. I followed Liverpool at the time and was listening to it on the radio. The police lost control of the crowd flow, resulting in overcapacity at the ground and the fatal crush. The construction of high wire pens prevented the fans from either moving sideways along the terraces or escaping onto the pitch. Ninety-six fans, mostly standing at the front, died as a result of being crushed against the high security fences around the pitch from which the victims could not escape. An inquest eventually concluded that the supporters were unlawfully killed due to grossly negligent failures by police and ambulance services to fulfil their duty of care to them. It was clear at the time that the Bournemouth-Leeds match had to be managed with public safety in mind first, followed by close control of the hooligans who just wanted violence.

The senior officer in charge of policing the match was Superintendent Umbridge. He was a strict disciplinarian, bombastic with a fiery, forthright approach. I was given the job of organising the whole of Bournemouth CID into a prisoner handling unit. The idea for the entire weekend was for uniformed officers to be out on the street maintaining order whilst all those arrested would be brought into the central lockup at Bournemouth where the CID would take over dealing with the prisoners. The uniformed bobby could then return to the street without being out of action for hours. At a meeting a few days before the match, Superintendent Umbridge had requested HQ to provide more officers. He believed that due to intelligence reports, there was likely to be wide-spread disorder. While we were given some support from outside forces such as our neighbours in Hampshire, he did not get the numbers he felt he needed. He was shortly to be proved right.

The fireworks started with a bang on the Friday night. Thousands of Leeds fans arrived through the evening, catching us on the hop. Fights started breaking out in pubs around the town, and large numbers of young men roamed about looking for trouble. One large group of about a hundred and fifty marched down the main road to the sea front chanting, stopping all the traffic, and climbing over cars full of frightened occupants. Twenty uniformed officers in shirt sleeve order, carrying no more than their short wooden truncheons, confronted the mob at the Exeter Road fly-over, near the sea front. The officers formed a thin blue line across the road while being pelted with cans, bottles and other missiles. Small groups from the mob rushed at the police line then retreated to the safety of the riotous horde before repeating the performance. These groups started to get bigger and more daring, and it looked like the small band of police officers was going to be overwhelmed. Fortunately, and due to good planning, at the rear of the police line was a police video operator accompanied by a still photographer who captured all the action. Just as things were beginning to look like they were going pear-shaped, a two-tone police siren sounded coming to the assistance of the gallant twenty. Simultaneously, the inspector in charge ordered his small band to charge the mob. I have never seen anything like it. Twenty policemen charged the 150 rioters who broke and ran in every direction and dispersed. We were all fully stretched that night as shop windows were broken and numerous acts of violence committed, mainly on Bournemouth residents. The cells were full – about thirty prisoners – and it was only the day before the match!

The next day, Saturday, started quietly but it was clear that it wouldn't stay that way for long. The football ground was then called 'Dean Court' before the current sponsorship virus struck, which led to old stadia being renamed after companies and corporations with little historical attachment to the locality; it is now known as the Vitality Stadium after a sponsorship deal, but most locals still call it Dean Court. The ground was on my patch of Boscombe, hence my being saddled with the prisoner-handling job. Superintendent Umbridge was insistent that the ground capacity would not be exceeded under any circumstances. This had been the problem at Hillsborough in Sheffield, and he was clearly not going to let the same thing happen in Bournemouth. We had received intelligence reports that a number of forged tickets were in circulation, so we could be in a situation where the ground capacity had been reached, but with legitimate ticket holders locked out. The problem of legitimate ticket holders being refused admission, the lack of sufficient police officers to deal with the crowds, and the aggressive violent behaviour of a substantial number of supporters already happening made the likelihood of a riot almost a certainty. The ground capacity for the stadium is now 10,700 seated but back in 1990 it was more like 14,000. Dean Court was not the size of ground intended to host such big teams as Leeds United, and especially for the last and most important match of the whole season being held on a Bank holiday weekend. The scene was set for confrontation.

We didn't have to wait long. The capacity for the ground was reached an hour before kick-off and then it started. Uniformed officers came under missile fire from increasingly large groups of men and youths. Stones, tree branches, bottles and anything else to hand were thrown at the police. Superintendent Umbridge who was commanding from inside the ground now deployed his Police Support Units (PSU). These officers were kitted out in flame-proof overalls, with synthetic armour in certain areas as well as a helmet with visor. They carried a round shield and a long baton. The officers were normal beat or patrol officers trained to national standards to carry out this kind of duty from time to time. They operated in units of twenty constables, two sergeants and one inspector. All officers in England and Wales work to the same methodology, so that different police forces can interact and support each other on national events. These units were supplemented with video and still camera operators whose task was to record what happened. The still photographer takes photos which are superior for identifications to be made, the video operator provides the moving pictures which show the intent and actions of those filmed. The police photographers had also been busy before the trouble started, taking passive shots of everything and everybody. This type of photography, taken when people are at their ease and without deliberate face coverings, can be used to help identification later when some of the same people cover their faces with hoods and scarves as they are engaged in violence and disorder.

As the trouble worsened, the volume of missiles increased and the numbers of what I can only describe as rioters swelled into the hundreds. At one stage it looked like the uniformed (PSU) officers would be overwhelmed, but they stood their ground valiantly. I noticed one odd thing in that the rioters ran past some police officers and special constables who were wearing the traditional uniform, and hurled missiles over their heads at the police in their more aggressive looking riot clothing. The day was saved when all six of our mounted officers – on loan from Thames Valley – charged into the rioters and sent them flying like skittles. The PSUs followed up by charging smack into the disorganised mob and gradually dispersed them. A pack of snarling police German shepherd dogs completed the mopping up. The uniformed officers had saved the day in the confidence that Superintendent Umbridge would support whatever action they felt necessary, to prevent the rioters from gaining access to the ground. The football match – yes, there was a football match – proceeded after a short delay. Leeds United won and were promoted to Division One; AFC Bournemouth lost and were relegated to the Third Division.

With much to celebrate, the Leeds fans invaded the town, drank many pubs dry and continued with the rampage which they had started the previous evening. Shop windows were smashed, peoples' heads were smashed and the mob got smashed. A great pile of deck chairs which had been made ready for the sedate summer visitors were burned, and many of the pedalos and items for holiday makers to enjoy were damaged. The total cost of this mayhem exceeded a million pounds. That evening Superintendent Umbridge appeared on the television and in the national press vowing revenge and stating that we would hunt down every miscreant and come banging on peoples' doors. He also banged a lot of times on his office desk which nearly disintegrated with his rage, as he became blue in the face cussing HQ for failing to give him the numbers of police he had asked for.

The disorder peaked on the Saturday night. As Sunday dawned over a Bournemouth which resembled *Kristallnacht* (the Night of Broken Glass) in pre-war Germany, the Leeds fans gradually dispersed, or the decent majority of them just enjoyed the views and ice creams like other holiday makers. The bad guys were played out. Now it was the turn of the CID. All the prisoners arrested were interviewed, evidence amassed and over one hundred charged with a variety of offences. We made sure to get good full-length photographs of all those in custody which we would use later to check with CCTV footage, and still photographs from the various scenes of mayhem. It was obvious that we would need to commence a 'post incident investigation' to track down those not arrested at the time. I therefore deployed a small team of detectives to start securing all the CCTV footage from shops, pubs and public places. Superintendent Umbridge demanded that all the disorder be subject to a post incident investigation. HQ CID did not altogether agree but were pushed into it by the chief constable. This did not help Superintendent Umbridge's blood pressure, and his desk took more impacts from his fist which was now becoming quite tender. And yes, I got the job of trying to sort out this huge mess, and investigate all the various crimes, damages and assaults.

The events of that weekend were also played out to the nation by that modern phenomenon called the twenty-four-hour news service. Reporters from the BBC, ITV, and Sky News as well as a dozen newspapers had carried the story as their main leaders. The Dorset Police came under the national microscope from the usual army of armchair critics who can always point out what the police did wrong but are never heard from before any event takes place. To make matters worse I was at home the following Sunday when I received a phone call from my assistant chief constable which is a bit like an army lieutenant receiving a phone call from a general.

'Tony,' he said, 'have you seen the *Sunday Rag*, it seems we have arrested a man who gave a false name when arrested and he has been bailed from court in the false name. They are saying that the Dorset Police are not up to it and are going to go banging on peoples' doors, but will they be banging on the right ones?'

My heart sank. I could see us being ridiculed. It must have been one of my men who dealt with this miscreant. 'OK, sir, I'm on it.'

I shot out and bought the paper; in fact, I bought all the papers. Yes, there it was on the front page, a youth outside Bournemouth Magistrates Court punching the air in triumph with his fist as he was released from the court cells. The action of the Dorset Police letting this man slip through the net was made great play of, as the press love to criticise us and quickly forget the valour which is shown on a daily basis. I went into Bournemouth police station and found the case papers for this individual. I read his personal descriptive form which is completed on every prisoner after they are charged. I remember the man was called Shaun Broke but noticed that entered on the criminal record form was the description of a tattoo on his arm with the name 'Darren'. Either this was the name of his gay lover or it was his own name and my dozy officer had missed the obvious. I gave the detective in question a ring that Sunday morning and called him in. We went through the case; his details had been checked by sending a police officer to his address in Leeds. They were told that Shaun Broke was in Bournemouth watching the game, and yes, he did live at the address given to the police. The problem was that it was not Shaun Broke who had been arrested. Obviously, a friend of his was using his identity. Luckily for us the real offender had obligingly provided us with his first name in the form of the tattoo and checks with the associates of Shaun Broke quickly revealed the true identity of the offender. The detective who dealt with the case was ashamed at his mistake and knew everyone else would know he had fallen down on the job. He was a good hard-working man; I didn't need to point out what a crass cock-up he had made. I didn't report him to face any disciplinary proceedings; he had just made a mistake; it happens. On the wall above my desk and throughout my career was pinned something I have always lived my detective career by, the inspirational words of a great American President, Theodore Roosevelt. In his speech 'The Man in the Arena' he emphasised that it is the people who strive and work hardest, who will also, from time to time, make mistakes. Darren's victory salute was short lived but our embarrassment lingered a little longer.

Having been instructed to carry out an investigation I had to discuss with my bosses the size of the team, support and budget. After some infighting between commanders I was allocated twelve officers, six uniform and six CID. I chose two detectives who I had worked with at Weymouth, as well as some very good local officers I knew. I have always chosen the best. We also had use of a mini version of HOLMES to help catalogue the sheer numbers of suspects and victims. I had the privilege of giving the operation a name, and being a history buff, and knowing that the Yorkist King Richard III used the emblem of a white boar which is used in York to this day, and that Leeds United football ground was situated in Boar Lane, 'Boar Hunt' it was to be.

We were fortunate in that a detective superintendent from the West Midlands, who had already led an investigation of this type, took the trouble to travel down to Dorset and give my team a morning's lecture on the 'ins and outs' of a post incident investigation, involving photographic and video evidence. Together with a couple of my men we visited 'Operation Carnaby' which had been set up by the Metropolitan Police in March 1990, when over a 100,000 people (by some estimates twice that) had rioted over Margaret Thatcher's attempt to bring in a poll tax. The operation was involved in identifying rioters by CCTV and photographs and bringing them to justice. I also spoke to John Revell, the Branch Crown Prosecutor and he assigned two CPS lawyers who advised on procedures, points to prove and general evidential matters throughout. It was always my practice to work closely with an assigned CPS lawyer on complicated enquiries.

So with the team assembled, and legal procedures understood, it was time to get moving. The first job was to gather in and secure all the CCTV and still photographs we could get from public and private sources. My first big problem was the press. The events of that May Day weekend

The secretary to Mr. Vivian Prins is led from an office above Hambros Bank in Charterhouse Street by the author, PC Nott. This was one of eleven letter bombs directed at Jewish-run businesses in the city of London on 10 November 1972. (With thanks to the *Daily Mail* and *London Evening Standard*)

The author alongside a BLMC Austin Allegro panda car c.1973; probably one of the worst cars ever built in Britain.

Crab fishing boats moored in the picturesque harbour of Weymouth. (*Reproduced courtesy of Weymouth BID*)

Peter and Monica Taylor on their wedding day in the 1950s. They would be happily married for twenty-seven years.

The Costa del Sol Hotel, Sea Road, Boscombe; the home of Peter and Monica Taylor.

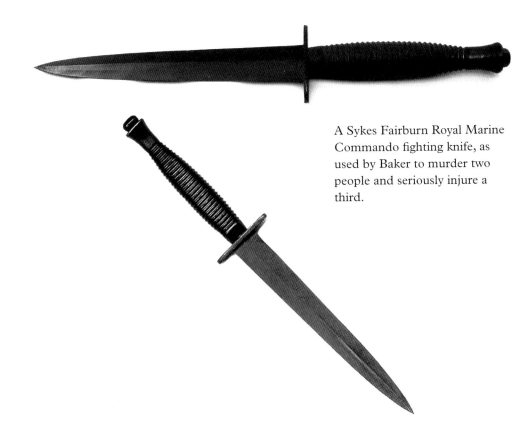

A Sykes Fairburn Royal Marine Commando fighting knife, as used by Baker to murder two people and seriously injure a third.

Iford Lane, Bournemouth. Old Bridge Road, where Mr Rattue was stabbed, can be seen on the right.

The front page of *The Sun* on Tuesday, 29 July 1986.

Exeter Road,
Bournemouth,
May 1990. The
Thin Blue Line.

The Thin Blue
Line draw
truncheons whilst
under missile fire
from bottles and
cans.

The Thin Blue
Line attacks.
(*Image kindly
provided by Karen
Woodstock-Jones*)

Outnumbered and under armoured. The Dorset Police, with help from Hampshire and Thames Valley, struggle to prevent an invasion of the stadium and thus avoiding the consequences with which we have all become too familiar. (*Reproduced courtesy of the* Bournemouth Echo. *Photograph by Duncan Lee*)

This officer has been hit with a brick, causing concussion, bruising and bleeding. (*Reproduced courtesy of the* Bournemouth Echo. *Photograph by Duncan Lee*)

The line holds – just. (*Reproduced courtesy of the* Bournemouth Echo. *Photograph by Duncan Lee*)

The quiet suburban street of Boscombe East; scene of the murder of Mr Geoffrey du Rose.

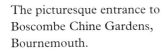

The picturesque entrance to Boscombe Chine Gardens, Bournemouth.

Boscombe Chine Gardens near the scene of the murder of Paul Bradshaw.

Churchill Gardens, Boscombe. It was from a flat near here where Halilowski and Grey set out to kill Michael Pearson.

Veronica Mary Packman, also known as Carole Anne Packman. (*Reproduced with the kind permission of Samantha Gillingham*)

Veronica Packman, Russell Packman (aka Causley) and Samantha Gillingham (née Packman). (*Reproduced with the kind permission of Samantha Gillingham*)

The tree lined, quiet, suburban area of Ipswich Road, Bournemouth; the home of the Causley family. The house where the murder took place has deliberately not been shown.

Bournemouth Central Police Station, as visited by Russell Causley when he reported his wife missing in 1985.

Causley's nemesis: (L-R) the author, DC Adrian Hugill, DC Paul Donnell, DS Chris Stone, DS Steve Rawles, Det. Supt. Pete Jackson.

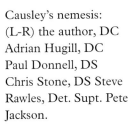

had been televised by SKY TV, ITV and the BBC. All the
major newspapers had also carried the story with a lot of
good photographs of violent disorder which we needed for
the investigation. On advice from the CPS I wrote to all the
news outlets and received almost the same reply, which was
that I could only have their 'journalistic material' if I had a
court order. So within several weeks of the riots a hearing
was arranged at Bournemouth Crown Court where I made
application for all the photographs and video recordings,
including broadcast and non-broadcast material. I also made
the case that the defence may want sight of the material,
which impressed His Honour Judge Giles Best enormously.
After I had appeared in the witness box to explain why the
police needed the material, the judge agreed there was a
case to answer, and asked the nine or more media groups if
they wished to make a defence. Eight of them acceded to the
police request and agreed to hand over all their photograph
and video footage. One organisation, the BBC, the only
publicly funded body by the British tax payer, refused to
hand anything over and mounted a defence. I am glad to
say that Judge Best ruled in our favour and the press were
ordered to hand over all the material. So on top of the fifty
hours or more video we had gathered, we now had a whole
lot more.

The incidents in and around Bournemouth that weekend
involved several pockets of violence. One was the Friday night
on the flyover, a second was outside the ground before kick-
off and there were several smaller scenes, as well as individual
crimes of robbery, damage and assaults to investigate. It took
a couple of months of work before we managed to identify
about ninety individuals who were core offenders, in that
they were seen to commit clear offences of throwing objects
at the police or assaulting people and could be identified on
film or photograph. We gave each suspect a target number
and tracked them through the large volume of film and
photographs we had. It was clear that several offenders
were involved in the violence at the flyover on Friday and
were again spotted throwing missiles outside the ground on
the Saturday. As this slow process dragged on, I was under

pressure from HQ CID to wrap the job up and get back to catching burglars, and from senior uniform officers to move faster and start feeling collars. Needless to say, I plodded on at my own speed; how else was I to get the evidence which would stand up in court, other than doing it deliberately and meticulously? I wasn't actually popular with anyone. Luckily, I had a good team; one officer, Dave Wilkie, put together the most superb trail of evidence from cameraman or CCTV pod, to final evidence copy to be shown to a suspect. This is called 'continuity of the exhibit' or 'chain of custody' and while it may sound boring, without it, a defence brief will drive a coach and horses through the case. One of the uniformed officers, Peter Staplin, a former Royal Marine, is worth a mention. He became known as 'Hawkeye' as he had an uncanny knack of identifying suspects in numerous parts of the video footage over and over again, often spotting targets missed by other officers on numerous viewings. This kind of observational keenness is a rare and valuable skill. My team was made up of officers with a range of skills from the quiet and methodical to the creative and off the wall and all that lies between; all the ingredients needed to make a good team.

After about six weeks the whole team went to West Yorkshire and split into four groups. We toured every police station we could and managed to identify about forty-five or so suspects by name. The West Yorkshire CID also had a good network of police informants. Certain ones were given discreet showings of the video and photographs that we had, and a lot of identifications were made from these sources. In order to protect the informants' identity, we made sure to visit the local police stations where these suspects lived. Then local beat officers were shown the photographs and video, who in turn provided the formal identification, thus removing the informant from the equation. Having made these identifications, we returned to Bournemouth where arrest packages were prepared.

Bill Ball, a uniformed constable stationed at Boscombe, was a football intelligence officer (FIO) whose special area of responsibility was AFC Bournemouth. Football intelligence officers are found in every police force in the country and are assigned to specific league football clubs in their areas. It is their business to know and monitor all their local trouble makers and assist the FIO in other forces when their teams meet. They are a great resource and have contributed enormously to the prevention and detection of football-related violence and disorder. Following the large-scale disorder, Bill contacted the football intelligence officers throughout the country and personally visited counties where there were known to be large numbers of Leeds supporters where he showed them our package of suspects; further identifications were made. The FIOs have their own network and keep in touch with each other on a daily basis; such an intelligence-gathering tool is essential to the police not only in detecting crime and disorder but being able to anticipate it and put in places measures to prevent it from happening.

It is the nature of criminals and those intent on causing trouble to engage in a whole series of criminal acts, becoming more brazen each time they do. They do not usually commit one offence and then stop. With this in mind and conscious of the fact that any perpetrators arrested may have engaged in criminal acts of violence, damage or disorder before they were finally caught, I ensured that the photographs of all the people arrested over that weekend were also examined against photographs of hooligans caught on camera engaged in violent disorder and other offences on the Friday and Saturday. This proved fruitful as the team identified about twelve on our video footage from the photographs of those arrested. For example, one of the suspects who was seen engaged in violent disorder on the flyover on Friday night was arrested for theft from a car the following day. When the cell block photograph taken of him when arrested for theft was checked against the most prolific trouble-makers, he was spotted throwing missiles at the police.

The local press was very keen to keep abreast of our developments as the arrest phase would be good news. I had a very good relationship with Mark Jones, the crime reporter on our local newspaper, the *Bournemouth Echo*. I had got to know Mark because he phoned me every morning to get updates on crime stories, and I always kept him in the loop on major crime investigations. I met Mark and one or two of his colleagues from time to time in a local wine bar. He would buy me lunch, which I always kept simple such as potato in its jacket or pizza and I made sure I bought the drinks. Even in the 1980s and 1990s it wouldn't have done to appear to be receiving favours, so I kept it even handed and always recorded it in my pocket book for transparency and accountability. I got on well with the local press; Mark (and his successors, Julie McGee and Jane Reader) because I laid out what I wanted and what I would give in return. I wanted to project a good image of the Dorset Police so that the public were reassured and felt their local council tax was being well spent, and I also wanted free advertising in their newspaper to circulate the descriptions of suspects, stolen property and give crime prevention advice. In return, I would keep nothing from them and give them good and comprehensive crime stories as they developed. I was clear with Mark that I would never mislead him but was firm that if I shared a confidence with him (and Julie and Jane later) I did not want it published until I was ready for it to be. The reason for this was that I wanted to maintain my integrity but could not endanger an investigation by the press releasing some vital fact and then losing the case on a technicality. Mark asked me whether he could cover the story with a photographer when the day came. It seemed a good idea to me. Superintendent Umbridge would be happy, his promise to go knocking on the doors of the guilty would have been fulfilled, and I thought it was a good deterrence message to send out to hooligans in general. I told John Homer at HQ CID what I had planned and he agreed with my rationale. I asked him to let Superintendent Umbridge know.

Just before the start of the football season in late July, the team returned to Milgarth Street police station in Leeds, West Yorkshire, to commence the arrest of our targets. I set up camp in the detective inspectors' office and the West Yorkshire Police gave us a large number of police officers to go to the various addresses and arrest the suspects. My small group was formed into six interview teams of two men each, who would interview their nominated targets as they were arrested. The whole thing resembled a sausage machine, suspects were arrested and searches of their houses bore fruit. Clothing, much of it garish, was recovered with the suspect, and the clothing seized clearly matched what they were wearing on the day as shown on the photographs or CCTV we had recovered from the press. They were then interviewed by my team and West Yorkshire officers helped in their subsequent documentation before court and bail procedures. The operation went swimmingly; some suspects ran off but were apprehended shortly after. Occasionally we had the wrong address because the suspect had just moved, but they were tracked down pretty quickly to their new abode and, on one rare occasion, the suspect was at work. Mark Jones was covering the story for the *Bournemouth Echo* and had some good shots of hooligans being brought to the police station with blankets over their heads. The local television also turned up and filmed me as I briefed the arrest teams at 6 am; the press coverage was excellent. Everything was going so well; that is until the phone went.

It was answered by DI Ackroyd. 'It's for you, Tony; Superintendent Umbridge.'

I took the phone. 'Hello, sir,' I cheerily said.

'How's it going, Notty?' he asked.

'Great, sir, we've got most of them in. One's made off through some neighbours' gardens, but they've got him cornered. We have had a couple of blanks which officers are rechecking, but everything is going well. We've got about twenty-eight in so far.'

'Great,' he said, 'I'll inform the press,' and immediately rang off.

'Oh,' said I to an empty phone, 'you don't know then!' It seemed that HQ CID had not passed the message I had asked them to a month earlier.

Not more than a minute passed before the phone went again. DI Ackroyd passed it to me. 'Superintendent Umbridge again.'

'Hello, sir.' This time not so cheerily

'NOTT,' came a demented shout. 'HAVE YOU GOT JONES WITH YOU?'

I said, 'I thought you knew,' and before I could respectfully say 'sir' the phone went click. I swear the plastic telephone receiver melted in my hand; I could almost feel the fiery breath coming down the phone. I replaced the receiver, feeling embarrassed and deflated from what I thought was a good operation.

DI Ackroyd said, 'Bit abrupt.'

'Yes,' I said. 'He seems to think he was just about to score a goal for England when some upstart came from nowhere and toe punted it over the line to get on the score sheet.'

Then the phone went again. 'DCI Harrison,' said DI Ackroyd.

Peter Harrison was the jovial giant from my Weymouth days and now the detective chief inspector in Bournemouth.

'Notty, I've just witnessed a minor explosion' he was tittering as he said it. 'I was in Superintendent Umbridge's office when he phoned you. Didn't you tell him you had the press with you?'

I immediately spluttered, 'HQ CID said they were going to tell him, it's not my fault.'

He tittered again. 'Notty, you've whipped the carpet from under his feet, he had his best uniform on to face the press, he was expecting the glory, now you've grabbed it from him at the last moment. You're in the shit now,' and he laughed a deep laugh which came from way down in his belly. I felt much better after that conversation.

When I returned to Bournemouth a day or two later, I found that I had already been forgiven. Superintendent Umbridge was now working on a conspiracy theory involving rivalry between HQ CID and the territorial divisions, and I was dropping out of the frame. He was one of those old-fashioned martinet characters who could dish out the almightiest bollockings but tended not to hold a grudge.

The investigation team amassed a huge number of photographs and video footage, some forty hours of it. All this had to be viewed several times, catalogued, indexed and stored. As well as the meticulous Dave Wilkie, I had

John Gadd, a civilian video technician on the team who normally worked at headquarters. They worked for weeks on what was mind-numbingly boring, but essential work in preserving and clarifying the exhibits required for the trial and the room full of photographs and video footage which was not used in evidence. This is referred to as 'unused material' and although the police do not wish to use it, the defence may find something in it of value for their clients. It is essential therefore, that all this material is made available to the defence. It occupied a whole room at headquarters and defence solicitors spent weeks poring over the material. I don't recall anything of significance being found, but it was important for me to have preserved everything for them.

About three months later, the suspects all appeared at Winchester Crown Court. There were several trials involving over fifty defendants in total. The largest trial involved twenty-six people of whom all but one was convicted. Almost all the remainder were convicted of either assault, violent disorder or some other similar public order offence. Custodial sentences were handed out to the majority of the hooligans which ranged from six to eighteen months' imprisonment. At the end of the trial of the twenty-six hooligans, the barristers involved, both prosecution and defence, presented the judge with the match ball, signed by them all, of course.

Operation 'Boar Hunt' was one of the last major investigations into football related violence that I can remember. Perhaps this type of behaviour had had its day, but also post incident investigations involving photographic and CCTV evidence made hooligans realise that there was a near certainty of them being caught.

CHAPTER 11

Murder on a Sunday Afternoon

For some reason, particular crimes can have a deep impact on you. What happened on Sunday 29 November 1992 was to be one of those days. It was the annual event of the 'Snow Queen Procession' in Christchurch where I lived. My wife and I were foster carers, and we had a young girl staying with us at the time. The procession started at about 6 pm but our little charge had to be there an hour or two earlier as she was taking part as a 'snow flake'. My wife asked me to slide off work early to help. I worked long hours and felt I was owed a shorter day. I was weekend cover in Bournemouth and thought I would take advantage of the quiet Sunday afternoon. I took my police radio home with me as you just never know what might happen.

It was a typical November day, grey and just enough rain to make everything cold and wet. I was walking out of the house with my wife and our temporary little princess at about 4 pm when I received a call on the radio. It was Detective Sergeant Mick Perrett, another rugby player with an acid wit, always taking the mickey out of his colleagues with an impish grin; but not today. He told me that a man had been stabbed with a carving knife and the offender was on the run in Boscombe East, an area of substantial mainly detached houses. This area is only five minutes from where I lived. By the time I arrived Mick was at the scene which was a detached house with a garden backing onto some shops. The suspect had run up a nearby road almost into the arms of the first uniformed police officer to arrive. The suspect brandished a six inch carving knife at the officer who stopped and attempted to speak to him. Just then by sheer bad luck a young woman drove along the road and stopped behind the knife man who was in the middle of the road. He then swung around, got into the passenger seat of her vehicle and ordered her to drive off with the knife at her throat.

The woman drove the vehicle at the man's command for thirty-six miles until it ran out of petrol in the adjoining county of Wiltshire. The Dorset Police firearms incident response vehicle had managed to catch up with the hijacked car and had remained on its tail with two tone horns blaring and blue lights flashing for many miles. When the hijacked vehicle pulled to the side of the road the two firearms officers coolly alighted from their vehicle and trained their guns on the suspect. Faced with the daunting appearance of two heavily armed and equipped policemen, with a no-nonsense attitude, the suspect immediately dropped his weapon and lay on the road as instructed. That was it, suspect arrested, knife with bloodstains of the victim on the blade recovered in his possession; it's all over then.

Well, no, actually; the tragedy was just beginning for Heather du Rose and her family. Her husband Geoffrey, a physical education teacher, had been repairing his guitar in an upstairs bedroom of his home earlier that afternoon. His twelve-year-old son was downstairs and his fifteen-year-old son was playing football with his mum watching him at a sports field nearby. Mr du Rose heard a noise in his back garden and looked out of the window. He saw a youth crashing through his back fence and running through his garden. He ran downstairs and gave chase. Being a fit man, he soon caught up with the intruder and as he was drawing level, the youth took a long carving knife from a make-shift cardboard sheath taped to his forearm, turned and stabbed Mr du Rose in the abdomen. Mr du Rose staggered back to his house where his twelve-year-old son did his best to staunch the bleeding with kitchen towelling and phoned the emergency number for an ambulance.

Mr Du Rose was rushed to hospital and the medical team fought like lions to save him. He survived for two days. The knife had penetrated his liver, kidney and spleen, and despite many blood transfusions, he succumbed after a valiant fight. The blood would just not coagulate. It was his son's sixteenth birthday. Mr du Rose was a loving husband and father with a talent for making classical guitars. He was devoted to helping children at the local Cub pack, and also the underprivileged youngsters he introduced to the Duke of Edinburgh's Award Scheme.

The killer, still in his teens, had experienced a completely different life from the family he had devastated. Just prior to the stabbing he had stolen a canister of lighter fuel from a newsagent shop behind the family house. In his bid to escape he had broken through a fence at the back of the shop after he had been seen stealing the lighter fuel. He carried the carving knife because he later claimed he lived in a violent environment. In fact, the youth had already got murder on his mind. He admitted later that he was on his way back to the foster unit he was living in to stab his roommate with whom he had had a number of disagreements. He came from a broken family with a drunken and abusive father, so he and his sister ran away from the father and lived with his mother; but that didn't work out either. His barrister told the court that on one occasion he left his local authority care home and walked seven miles to visit his mother, but at the conclusion of the visit she wouldn't give him a lift back to the care home and so he had to walk back. He was troublesome at school and was expelled owing to his behaviour. He was involved in fighting and drug taking, which resulted in him amassing a long criminal record. The jury took three and a half hours to arrive at their verdict, dismissing his plea that the crime was as a result of depression and drug taking; he was convicted of murder. He whistled and grinned as he was led from the dock having received the mandatory life sentence.

One of the interviewing officers, Detective Sergeant Bob Lee, described the killer as cold and emotionless with no regard for other decent members of society. Despite all that had happened, Heather du Rose displayed no bitterness or hatred and was heroic in the way she managed her family through the grief. This was a very close family, completely devastated by the crime; totally undeserving of what had happened and marked forever by it. She was a very go-ahead lady who wanted to see her husband's funeral as a true celebration of his life and not as a dark final event. She also wanted a white hearse, but national rules covering undertaker's vehicles prohibited this at the time.

I regularly briefed my divisional commander about the progress of the case and mentioned to him, what was then, an unusual request to have a white hearse for the funeral. Superintendent Umbridge was so moved by the lady's plight that he immediately determined to help. He personally made contact with the transport department and arranged to borrow a brand-new white van which had just been delivered to the Dorset Police HQ. The vehicle was to be used to take internal mail and other such material from station to station. Fortunately, it had not been emblazoned with Dorset Police markings. We obtained Mrs du Rose's acceptance that this vehicle was what she wanted, and the undertaker agreed to this unusual arrangement. Bob Lee and DC Sandra Robertson were the officers who closely worked with the family through the legal and emotional trials they had to go through and were both particularly caring and sensitive. They attended the funeral which they both took a major part in organising. For one day the unmarked Dorset Police van was used for an afternoon as a hearse and was driven by Detective Sergeant Lee, acting as unofficial undertaker. The funeral took place in Hampshire at the same church where Mr and Mrs du Rose had been married years before. I don't think the chief constable, nor indeed anyone else apart from Superintendent Umbridge and myself, ever knew what the van was used for. Since this sad day the rules governing undertaker's vehicles have changed and white hearses have become quite acceptable. Murder is sometimes exploited to entertain and amuse and presented in a clean detached manner by writers. It is in fact very messy, deeply traumatic and the victim's families never really fully recover. The phrase 'moving on' seems to be used too frequently. People can move on but it's never the same; they are changed for ever, as this brave family was.

CHAPTER 12

The Disappearance of Veronica: Russell Causley Part One

Somehow and with unseen assistance from the Goddess Fortuna, I was promoted to Detective Chief Inspector in October 1993. The Yugoslav Civil War was now in its third year, the phrase 'ethnic cleansing' had entered the lexicon and the western powers seemed impotent to do anything. It was only stopped after the Americans in their resurgence after the First Gulf War, entered the fray with all guns blazing. It was the US that knocked back the murderous forces of Slobodan Milosevic to save the lives of countless Bosnian Muslims. How soon was that forgotten?

I was at this time the crime manager at Bournemouth, and part of what was called the 'command team.' This group was headed by a chief superintendent who had a uniformed superintendent in charge of all operational uniform patrol tasks, a uniformed superintendent in charge of all police personnel matters, a senior civilian administrator doing all the vital admin stuff and me in charge of all crime. It always seemed odd to me that the senior police officer responsible for the investigation of crime was the most junior in rank in the command team. Still, enough of that. As the crime manager, I had 20,000 crimes a year to worry about as well as the rising star, Tony Rogers, who was now a detective superintendent and introducing a new concept called 'intelligence-led policing'. This caused massive changes in the way the police did their business and altered us from a reactive stance to one of aggressively and proactively targeting criminals through the use of intelligence. A constant statistic over the years has been that seven percent of criminals commit sixty-five percent of recorded crime. It is therefore much more efficient to target those repeat offenders, than walking aimlessly around in circles.

In the early spring of 1994, while engaged with these heady matters of strategy and organisational efficiency and at the same time overseeing numerous serious investigations, Detective Sergeant Chris Stone wandered into my office. Chris is a taciturn, no-nonsense type of guy with a serious countenance and a very dry sense of humour.

'There's a DS Fallah from Guernsey coming over tomorrow, sir,' he said. 'He's investigating some sort of possible insurance fraud involving a bloke called Russell Causley. Apparently, he was living in Bournemouth and might have some connections, or friends here.'

'OK, Chris' I said. 'Look after him, will you?' It is customary for police officers to look after their counterparts from other forces when they visit to help with using phones, computers, intelligence checks and all other resources that visiting investigators need. The visit is usually concluded with a visit to the pub and the swapping of war stories known as 'swinging the lamp' as is the custom with police officers across the country, and as I was later to discover, the world.

The next day Chris came into my office and told me of the visit.

'What visit?' I asked, having forgotten already having been overwhelmed with the new day's continuing flood of crime, problems and disasters.

'The DS from Guernsey.'

'Oh, yes; how did it go?'

Chris then told me that earlier that month, (October 1993), a man called Russell Causley had reportedly fallen overboard from a yacht off the coast of Guernsey. A sea and land search was launched, but he was not found, nor was a body recovered. The remainder of the crew, his girlfriend Patricia Causley, and two other people had put the boat into St Peter Port, Guernsey. Detective Sergeant Fallah, when speaking to the survivors, had become suspicious. He made enquiries after they had left with the local ferry company and discovered that Russell Causley was booked as a passenger on the outgoing ferry. He had in fact accidently blurted out his name when buying the ticket. While it could have been an advance booking, DS Fallah trusted the ship's manifest to be an accurate record of passengers actually travelling on the day on the outgoing ship.

I was confused about the names. 'She's his girlfriend but they're both called Causley.'

'Yes,' he said. 'He changed his name from Packman to Causley after he met her. He's got an address in Ipswich Road in Bournemouth; his wife Veronica apparently went missing from there about nine years ago. DS Fallah doesn't know what happened to her, but said he thought it had been reported to the police at the time.'

Chris then told me that having concluded his investigations in Bournemouth without finding Causley, DS Fallah had gone on to the Kent area where he had some reason to believe that Causley was living.

I said casually, 'Better check out the misper [missing person] file, Chris.'

A day or two later, Chris came back into my office, 'I can't find a misper file for Veronica Packman, Russell Causley's wife. Apparently, it's been destroyed as she subsequently came into Bournemouth police station to say she was alive and well. But I've made some preliminary enquiries to ascertain her whereabouts but can find no trace of her.'

I remember thinking, 'Oh, no, not another one.' I knew how much work and difficulties could lie ahead if this woman wasn't found quickly.

I said, 'We'll have to bottom this out one way or the other; you'd better keep with it.'

DS Fallah in the meantime was busy tracing any known relatives of Causley and he located Samantha Gillingham, Russell Causley's daughter. He found her in a state of grief because she believed her father was dead as a result of the sailing accident; she would find out later that this was a cruel deception which damaged her deeply.

Within weeks of the visit of DS Fallah, we learned that Russell and Patricia Causley had been arrested for fraud in Kent. Patricia had been followed by investigators to a local public house where she was seen to meet Russell and they were both arrested. Russell and Patricia, along with another associate in the crime, were charged with conspiracy to defraud the insurance company, with an amount in the region of £900,000. Russell was initially remanded in custody to Brixton Prison but later released on bail. Chris Stone teamed up with one of his detectives to assist in the enquiry. This was Paul Donnell who is about as different from Chris as chalk is from cheese in some respects. Whilst both were dedicated and professional investigators, Paul was gregarious, handsome, and a complete ladies' man. I once walked through a crowd of college girls with him whilst on an enquiry. Every head turned and sized him up, but not one glance in my direction, I'm afraid. However, underneath his suave exterior lurked a very competent detective.

In early 1994 and as a result of the good work by DS Fallah, Chris contacted Russell Causley's daughter Samantha Gillingham, nee Packman. She described her early life in which she painted a picture of her parents both of whom were professionals in the aircraft industry. They lived in and around Bournemouth, but on occasions worked for significant periods in Canada and Germany. Samantha recalled that she first met Patricia Causley in 1983 when she worked for her father in an insurance company he had established. Shortly after this Patricia sold her flat and moved into the family home in Ipswich Road, Bournemouth, where she lived as Russell's mistress. Bizarrely enough, Veronica, her mother, remained living in the matrimonial home (coincidentally similar to Taylor's mistress moving into the Hotel Costa del Sol). During this time Samantha's relationship with her father deteriorated and she described how he made both her mother and her bow down before him, and he also beat her physically. Russell had been arrested for assaulting his daughter when she was a teenager, but charges were subsequently dropped. She was taken temporarily into local authority care following these problems and experienced a number of difficulties in her own life around this time as she was growing up.

When Samantha returned to Ipswich Road, Patricia was still living with her father and mother and again bizarrely she would occasionally be looked after by Patricia when her mother and father were both away working. On either 11 or 15 June 1985 she recalled going to London with her father where they met Patricia for lunch. She could not remember seeing her mother that morning, but she did remember returning home that evening. She remembered seeing her mother's wedding ring on a kitchen worktop together with a note in her mother's handwriting saying she'd had enough and couldn't take any more. She went to her mother's bedroom, where she saw her mother's favourite red dress torn up and the wardrobe doors open. She remembered seeing her mother's Rolex wrist watch and expensive jewellery in the room. Her mother had disappeared, but her expensive jewellery and personal possessions had not! It was not until August of that year that her father decided to report his wife missing at Bournemouth police station. She went with him to the police station, and he told the police that £4000 or £5000 in cash was also missing from the house. Samantha's relationship with her father deteriorated, and he asked her to leave the house. She ended up sleeping rough and experienced all kinds of difficulties in her mid-teens. She made strenuous efforts to trace her mother but could not find her. The disappearance of her mother had a devastating impact on the young Samantha, from which after a time, and through her own strength of character, she managed to slowly recover.

Veronica's mother and brother were also traced in early 1994. They told Chris and Paul of how Veronica had met Russell in 1965 and married him shortly after when she was aged 20. Not long after the marriage they related how Russell had cut Veronica off from making further contact with them. They were aware through Veronica that Russell had made threats to 'chop them up with an axe' which resulted in an almost total loss of contact. They said that occasionally Veronica contacted them to complain that Russell had beaten her up, and on another that he had kicked their Alsatian puppy to death for causing a mess on the floor. It was only through Russell's solicitor that they learned of her disappearance. They were told a few months later that she had walked into the police station to declare herself alive and well by the same solicitor, but they had never heard from her again.

Chris and Paul then had to set about tracking down the original officers who dealt with the missing person report nine years earlier. The paperwork had been destroyed which was in accordance with accepted procedures at the time and the officer who took the report had since died. However, they managed to track down an inspector who had knowledge of the case. He told them to the best of his memory that the case was closed because the missing person, Veronica Packman, had come into Bournemouth police station with a child and reported herself alive and well. Living where and with whom he did not know, nor did he recollect if the person taking the report from the woman checked the missing person file against the photograph (if any) held by the police. The time of the alleged appearance of Veronica at Bournemouth police station was thought to be prior to Christmas 1985.

It had now become imperative to find Veronica Packman. Chris and Paul checked her doctor, bank, National Insurance, HM Inspector of Taxes as well as other public record offices. They contacted Immigration Departments in Canada, Germany and Italy. They made numerous enquiries throughout the aircraft industry internationally within the disciplines the Packmans' worked. They traced friends, neighbours and acquaintances of both Veronica and Russell in and around Bournemouth and world-wide. They drew a complete blank. One of the last recorded and perhaps most important sightings of Veronica was when she had visited her solicitors, Messrs Ward Bowie, in Bournemouth. She told her solicitor that she wished to commence divorce proceedings and sell the matrimonial home. After a lengthy discussion she was advised to establish what her husband's position was likely to be in any divorce and to book another appointment. This meeting took place on the 14 June 1985, the day before Russell Causley took his daughter to London after which they returned to Ipswich Road to find the torn dress and note on the bedside table. There was no trace whatsoever of Veronica Packman after 15 June 1985 anywhere on the planet; she had ceased to exist.

This now caused me considerable worry. With what was now known about Russell Causley: allegations of violence and controlling behaviour; possible legal proceedings leading to divorce; his tendency to engage in major criminal activity (the insurance fraud involved over £900,000); all this was leading to a bad mix. The case was still a missing person enquiry, but the time was shortening to a point, not too far distant, when the investigation may turn into one of suspected murder. Once that point was reached Russell and Patricia Causley would have to be treated as suspects and cautioned to not say anything before they were questioned. My years of experience taught me that those with something to hide would more often than not fall back on their entitlement to silence, or only give answers to specific points without answering secondary questions.

There was only one thing for it; Chris and Paul had to travel to Kent to speak to Russell Causley who had, after a passage of time, been released on bail pending his trial for fraud. The three of us sat down, went through the case in detail and all agreed that the time to treat Russell as a suspect had not yet arrived. After all, perhaps he now knew of his wife's whereabouts; maybe she had changed her name and was living happily somewhere in the world and had slipped through the net; or maybe not. If, when answering questions about his wife's disappearance nine years earlier, those answers are found to be lies; then that would be of enormous significance at any trial. Keeping an open mind but remaining objective is the balance the detective must maintain.

CHAPTER 13

'I fear for my mother':
Russell Causley Part Two

On 1 June 1994, over three months after DS Fallah breezed into the Bournemouth CID office, Detective Sergeant Stone and Detective Constable Donnell went to Cooks Broom, Mount Pleasant Lane, Lamberhurst, Kent, where they saw Russell and Patricia Causley who were both on bail awaiting trial for the life insurance fraud. They had moved there from Ipswich Road in Bournemouth having sold the house some months previously. The officers explained that they were reviewing the missing person report of Veronica Packman and were seeking her current whereabouts. Paul got the distinct impression that Russell wrote them off as a pair of carrot crunchers from Dorset; he described him as bombastic and full of self-confidence. When he heard the reason for their visit, he told them he wanted to tape record the conversation and put a tape cassette into a recorder he had in the room. The meeting lasted a couple of hours during which time Russell told the officers that he had had little contact with his wife since she disappeared. He told them that the last time he saw his wife was when she disappeared on 15 June 1985. He said that he had received a letter and telephone call from her in 1989 or 1990 when he was in Grob, Germany, when she had asked him if he was still with Patricia. He told Chris and Paul that he did not ask his wife about her circumstances, nor did she volunteer any information. He believed she had traced him through the aircraft industry, which he said and which we later confirmed, was not a difficult thing to do. It was quite a close intimate group. He was asked if he still had the letter which she had sent to him but claimed it had been destroyed along with a number of other papers when he left Ipswich Road. He said the letter contained a number of questions from her about his domestic life with Patricia. He believed she had a boyfriend who drove a Porsche, and that his daughter Samantha may have met him. This was later checked with Samantha, and she said that she had never met such a person and re-affirmed she had not seen or heard from her mother since mid-June 1985. Russell did say that a suitcase, toiletries and £7000 cash had been taken when she left. He was reluctant to talk about family relationships but said that Veronica did not want to speak to her parents despite his endeavours to encourage contact.

At the conclusion of this meeting, and typical of Chris and Paul, they drove a short distance from Cooks Broom before they pulled over into a lay-by and meticulously recorded the conversation in their note books. This may seem insignificant, but notes made as soon after an event are likely to be the most accurate as the events being recalled are still fresh in the minds of the makers. This kind of integrity in a major police enquiry is of paramount importance and I frequently used this episode as an example of professional record keeping to junior officers. It took them over an hour to write out their recollections of the meeting. At the end of their note writing and as they digested the conversation in full, Chris Stone said, 'What do you think?'

Paul replied, 'He's killed her, mate. He's killed her.'

So the game was afoot. Russell was maintaining that despite all the enquiries made, his wife was alive and well and living with a man with a Porsche. There was no proof that Veronica had sent him a letter, because he claimed that he had destroyed it when he left Ipswich Road and could not remember where it had been sent from. But, when he left the matrimonial home in Bournemouth, who else signed the deeds of sale? If the house in Ipswich Road had been in both names, what signatures were on the documentation? His certainly, but what about hers?

Enquiries were made with the office of H.M. Land Registry which revealed that the full ownership of the property was transferred to Russell from his wife Veronica in June 1990. A letter purporting to be from his wife was sent to Russell's solicitors which asked for the title of the property to be transferred to Russell, in view of the fact that she had received a substantial financial package from him as part of divorce proceedings. That same month, Russell instructed his solicitors to transfer the title deeds from the names R.S. Causley and C.A. Packman to that of R.S. and P.A. Causley. The initials C.A. Packman stand for Carole Anne Packman which is the name used by Veronica at Russell's request in the early stages of their relationship. Oddly enough, his sister was called Carole Anne! Subsequent examination of the signature C.A. Packman on the title deed transfer documents were compared by experts to the known real signatures of Veronica and shown to be a forgery. Both Russell and his girlfriend Patricia later admitted these were forgeries.

An obvious line of enquiry was to trace and speak to the friends of Russell and Veronica, many of whom worked in the aircraft industry. Chris and Paul worked wonders in contacting the vast majority of his friends and associates throughout the world. Friends were found who recounted conversations with Russell which took place after the disappearance of his wife. Some friends told the police that Russell had told them that she was living in Germany; other friends said that Russell had told them that she was in Switzerland, others Israel, and some friends mentioned Canada. Some added that he told them she had gone off with a rich man who drove a Porsche.

Amongst the friends traced were some who related conversations with Veronica about her intention to divorce her husband and sell the house. Some of these friends were aware of her intention to commence divorce proceedings through her solicitors. These conversations could be dated to early June 1985. There was little surprise about Veronica's ailing marriage as some had noticed suspicious bruising on her arms which she had tried to explain away. It was commonly believed that she was subject to domestic violence.

What also started to emerge was a picture drawn by all these friends and associates of a bombastic, arrogant man who used controlling behaviour over his wife and daughter. He also displayed dubious sexual tendencies which were corroborated by a number of people as the enquiry progressed. Despite the build-up of suspicion, we were desperately short of direct evidence.

During this time, Samantha was making appeals in the press for information which could lead to the discovery of her mother's whereabouts. This was both at local and later national level. These press articles stirred up some interest in the force and I received an unexpected visit from Superintendent G. Nicholls, a former professional footballer, with a burning drive to make it to chief constable. He had a face which always reminded me of the moon with two small craters for eyes. He worked for a department within headquarters and was keen to demonstrate to senior commanders that he had a firm grip on all major issues affecting the force. At this time, HQ CID dealt with murder enquiries and other very serious crimes while the CID on divisions dealt with most of the rest. There were tensions and rivalries between HQ departments and senior officers on territorial divisions, a mix which Superintendent Umbridge had been embroiled in a couple of years earlier. I related the extent of our enquiries to Superintendent Nicholls in the presence of Chris and Paul, but I made the mistake of suggesting that Russell Causley may well have murdered his wife and hidden the body. I received an immediate dressing down in the presence of the junior officers that I was exceeding my authority, and I was told 'this was a missing person enquiry and nothing else.' The sentence was punctuated with a cold stare.

For once, I was struck dumb by this quite humiliating attitude but could see in the dark crater-like eyes of my visitor the reason behind his outburst; I was becoming a career threat! He then walked out, without much further ado. Chris and Paul also looked shocked.

I said, 'This is a fucking murder enquiry.'

To which Chris said, 'Too right, it is.'

I then had to survive the wrath of Headquarters by not mentioning this enquiry while at the same time ducking from the divisional commander who also felt I was giving too much time to this investigation. During the fraud trial in March 1995 which related to Russell Causley's disappearing act from the yacht off the coast of Guernsey I made sure that Paul went up to London frequently to monitor the case. I remember the divisional commander having read a report on the fraud trial in the *Bournemouth Echo* speaking to me about it, and I foolishly displayed more knowledge about it than I should have.

He said, 'You know a lot about this case, Notty. You haven't got anyone on this full time, have you?'

'No, Guv,' I said, fully realising I had been a little economical with the truth, having had both Chris and Paul committed to this enquiry full time for months. I was lucky he didn't examine their expenses claims or my career may have come to a sudden halt. His main concern was using scarce resources on a 'missing person enquiry' when we were under pressure to meet targets in other quarters. I also got a lecture on obsession and what a bad thing it could be to be obsessed about a case. I'm sure he had just seen 'Les Misérables' and likened me to Inspector Javert. So I provided top cover whilst Chris and Paul carried on discreetly in the engine room getting the job done.

On 24 March 1995, Russell Causley was sentenced to two year's imprisonment for conspiracy to defraud and Patricia was given a suspended sentence. He went off to HMP Brixton and it was going to be downhill all the way from there. In April that year, not long after his conviction, a call was received at Bournemouth CID office concerning the disappearance of Carole Packman. It was one of those out of the blue phone calls policemen dream of. The call was from a reporter on the *Sunday Express*, who had crucial information to pass on; he had been contacted by a serving prisoner at HMP Rochdale. The prisoner had read the article he had written in the *Sunday Express* concerning the conviction of Russell Causley, and more importantly about the disappearance of his wife. The prisoner had something he wanted to tell the police but had been unable to make a direct contact and had asked the reporter to get the police to visit him.

Within twenty-four hours, Chris and Paul were at HMP Rochdale, pen in hand. The man they had gone to see was Michael Lomond. He was a small-time criminal who had been sent to prison because he had committed fraud in order to try and save his ailing bookmaker's shop. He told Chris that he had read an article in the *Sunday Express* called 'I fear for my mother' which featured an appeal by Samantha Packman asking for information about her mother's disappearance. He told Chris that he had shared a cell with Russell Causley, and they had told each other about the crimes they had committed. During these heart to heart chats, Russell made some disclosures to him about his wife. He remembered an occasion when during their confinement in their cell, a letter arrived for Russell which he did not open. Mr Lomond was intrigued as to why the letter remained unopened and challenged him about it. He said it was from his daughter (Samantha) and that they didn't get on very well; this, of course, was true. He later told Mr Lomond that when he was arrested for the fraud, he at first thought he was being arrested for killing his wife, and he was relieved that it was only for the fraud. He told him that after he had killed her, he arranged for two people to take her body to a cemetery but couldn't remember the name of it. When Mr Lomond brought up the subject again, Russell became violently angry and his face contorted, terrifying Mr Lomond. This led to an intervention by prison officers and the two prisoners were separated to different cells. He described Russell as someone who was subject to rapid and pronounced mood swings, who would sometimes stare at him in a really evil manner. It was a short while after their separation that he read the *Sunday Express* article and felt that he must in all conscience contact the police. He made a full written witness statement to Chris and Paul while in prison which was to cost him dear.

Before Mr Lomond was interviewed by Chris Stone, it was known that he had contacted the reporter at the *Sunday Express*. This caused me some concern because if he wanted first to sell his story to the press then his reliability as a witness would be brought into serious question. After all, was he just in it for the money? So called 'cheque book journalism' was very well known at this time and some sections of the press paid well for these types of stories. Enquiries were made with the reporter which showed the opposite: Mr Lomond did not ask for money; all he wanted were the contact details for Chris. Mr Lomond had tried to contact him direct, but in the newspaper article the officer's name was spelt incorrectly which is why he couldn't trace him and so contacted the journalist who wrote the article.

I met Mr Lomond sometime later, and I found him to be sincere and genuine. I fully believed his account despite the fact that the disclosure about two men taking a body to a cemetery seemed very odd, especially in the context of a murder. Again, it is incumbent on the detective to faithfully record what he is told, even though it may not make much sense at the time; not to engineer what he would like to hear. It is often when as an investigation nears its conclusion that things fall into place and the picture on the jigsaw puzzle gradually becomes clearer.

We now, at last, had some real direct evidence to implicate Russell Causley in the murder of his wife, and to give substance to the wealth of circumstantial evidence gathered by Chris and Paul. The next step was obvious, Russell Causley and his girlfriend Patricia must be arrested and the facts as gathered during the investigation put to them for their comment. Chris, Paul and I sat together to discuss tactics. Now it was also time for me to reveal to my superiors the changed state of the enquiry. The first to know was the Head of Dorset Police, CID Chief Superintendent Donohoe. Desi, as he was known, was an old time CID officer. He was the son of two Irish itinerant hotel workers who came to Bournemouth in the 1930s looking for work. His grandfather was reputedly an IRA volunteer from the Irish Civil War and given an IRA funeral. He was about as politically incorrect as you could imagine but possessed a ruthless drive to see criminals brought to justice and ensured that those under his command carried that out. I outlined the case to him from the beginning. He grasped the job immediately, gave me full command of it with no HQ interference and backed whatever action we thought necessary. The game had changed. I did not want to swell the team at this stage. I have always been an advocate of small numbers of highly proficient investigators. When the time came to increase the size of the team, I would choose the best, from the best.

In early August 1995, Chris and Paul arrested Russell Causley at HMP Dorchester while he was serving his sentence for the insurance fraud. Patricia was also arrested at the same time. They were both questioned about the disappearance of Veronica and the account given to the police by Mr Lomond. They both declined to answer all police questions, but Russell did make a written statement under caution which he dictated to his solicitor. In this statement he admitted having shared a cell with Mr Lomond at HMP Brixton, and he related that they told each other about the crimes and frauds they had committed. He also agreed that he had received a letter from his daughter which remained unread which he said 'fascinated' Mr Lomond. He also said that he told Mr Lomond that he didn't get on with his daughter. However, on the issue of his ex-wife – he used that term three times – he said it was ludicrous to suggest he had two people carry her to a cemetery and denied telling him she was dead. He said that Mr Lomond talked a lot, which irritated him, and after an argument, Lomond banged on the cell door and asked the prison officers to move him to another cell. After these police interviews, Russell was returned to prison to continue serving his sentence. Both he and Patricia were bailed in relation to the murder enquiry.

Our next job was to submit all the paperwork to the CPS for experienced lawyers to study the evidence and make a decision regarding prosecution. The test used by the CPS is 'does the case have a realistic prospect of a conviction?' Going by the fact that our main evidence was from a convicted criminal and remembering well how in the Taylor case the word of Mr Matthews alone was insufficient, I did not hold out much hope.

CHAPTER 14

Déjà Vu All Over Again: Russell Causley Part Three

While preparing the case papers, Chris got another of those phone calls policemen dream about; this time from Patrick Murphy, a petty criminal who had recently been released from a short prison sentence at HMP Ford. He had spent some of his time in custody with Russell Causley. He had been told by one of his criminal associates that Causley, his cell mate, had been arrested for murder, which unsettled him. Murphy was a thief, but murder was another matter. He was the same age as Louis Matthews and not dissimilar in outlook; the whole thing made him uncomfortable. He decided to tell the police because he wouldn't have been able to live with himself, or so he later told us. He found the telephone number for Bournemouth CID, and after some initial difficulties got through to the man he needed – DS Stone. He downloaded to him all he knew about Causley. Chris came and told me straight after he had received the call. It was beginning to become like a dream, first lots of suspicion, but no direct evidence, now two prisoners willing to tell us about cell block confessions with Russell. Was this case now going too well?

What would be of paramount importance was to interview Mr Murphy with a clean untainted officer who had no knowledge of this case whatsoever. If Chris or Paul had gone to see him the first thing the defence, and in fairness the jury, could have thought, would be 'So what did they tell him before he made his statement?' This had to be so transparent as to be above reproach. I searched and found a detective from another division. This was John Crossland, a tall, fair and handsome man who exuded honesty and integrity from his very pores. I questioned him about his knowledge of this investigation and of the characters in it and it became clear to me that he had no inkling of this job whatsoever. I handed him a written brief establishing this fact, and I forbade him to speak to Chris or Paul. I then sent him off to London to interview Mr Murphy and take a statement from him. This is what he came back with: -

Mr Murphy, a man well into middle age, had been sentenced to five weeks in prison for driving a car whilst disqualified from driving. Because of his age and the length of the sentence, he was sent to HMP Ford – which was an open prison – in April 1995. There he met Causley, who was serving his sentence for the life insurance fraud, and they shared some interests in engineering. On one occasion Mr Murphy was talking to Russell about car engines and in particular a method of degreasing car engines by immersing them in acid. While talking about this process, Russell told him that his wife was called Carole, whom he had killed, and he had used acid to dissolve her body, but was unsure if all the bones had dissolved. He was interested in the new police technique of recovering DNA from any residue and seemed to be concerned about it. He said that she hadn't suffered because he had given her a shot of gas first, then suffocated her with a plastic bag over her head. He went on to tell Murphy that his girlfriend knew all about it, but she would never tell the police because she was as strong as a rock. He was confident that he was too shrewd for them (the police). He was also able to recall the name of a dishonest solicitor, who was one of Russell's co-accused in the life insurance fraud case. These conversations occurred whilst he and Russell walked around the perimeter wire, a fact noticed by another serving prisoner. Mr Murphy came to view Russell as cocky and arrogant. It was several months after Mr Murphy's release that he contacted the police and only after he had heard of Russell's arrest through the 'grapevine'. He had consulted his daughter before contacting the police because he needed and valued her opinion and reassurance that he was doing the right thing.

An advice file which contained all the witness statements reports and documentary evidence, as well as a full report on the case was then submitted to the CPS, which also included this new cell block confession. While this made the case slightly stronger, Murphy did not corroborate Lomond in detailed particulars and the chance of CPS going with it was, I felt, still slim. I was also uneasy about how Causley had apparently told him that he killed his wife with a shot of gas before suffocating her with a bag over her head. How could he administer the gas in the first place? It sounded as if it was right out of the film *Ten Rillington Place*. I wasn't hopeful. However, once again I was wrong and the CPS in the form of the Branch Crown Prosecutor John Revell said, 'I think we should give it a run.' This made me smile inside because this was an oft-used term by the police before the CPS came into being. In the past, where a case was weak and the chances of a conviction about fifty-fifty, it was sometimes considered by the police that it was better to let the court decide in public, rather than for men in suits behind closed doors to abandon prosecutions because they weren't completely water tight! John Revell was an outstanding crown prosecutor, quiet, thoughtful, always objective, and possessed with the guts to put cases to the crown court where there was a clear public interest need – this was one such instance.

In early February 1996, Russell Causley was re-arrested for the murder of his wife. He was questioned again about Veronica's disappearance and disclosures made by friends and acquaintances to the police, which he declined to answer. He was told about the statement made by Mr Murphy and the conversation about disposing of Veronica's body in acid to which he did reply both verbally and in writing. He was adamant that no such conversations occurred, and he could not remember meeting or talking with a prisoner at HMP Ford of that name. However, despite his denials, Chris and Paul made extensive enquiries among former prisoners and staff who had been incarcerated or worked with Mr Murphy and Russell and were able to prove that he was lying and they had indeed met. After questioning and when charged with the murder of his wife, he maintained that he did not kill her, and that she was still alive.

The enquiry team was now increased by several more detectives who helped track down further friends of Veronica and Russell. One of Russell's former colleagues in particular was able to tell the police that he believed that Russell and Patricia went to work in Canada in 1996 the year after Veronica's disappearance. He had heard through the aircraft workers' network that Patricia had been deported from Canada because she was caught using the identity and documentation of Veronica Packman! If this was so then Veronica's passport was being used by Patricia, inferring she was dead, or she would not need to use it. Any chance of Veronica being abroad was therefore highly unlikely as she clearly did not have her passport – Patricia Causley did. The Royal Canadian Mounted Police were able to provide evidence that Patricia Causley was deported from Canada a year after Veronica's disappearance having been caught impersonating her by the use of her passport. The use of Veronica's passport was damning; not only did it imply that Russell and Patricia Causley knew she was dead; it also blew a hole in his story that she had gone to Germany, Switzerland, Israel or any other foreign country for that matter.

Russell's parents were also traced with a view to asking them if they had had any contact with their daughter-in-law, and their views were sought on family dynamics. However, Russell's father was a strong character and exerted considerable influence over his wife; he refused to speak or cooperate with the police investigation. However, another family member let slip that there was an occasion when Russell and Patricia visited them and they had an argument. Angry exchanges were recounted and Russell was heard to shout at Patricia that 'he'd killed one wife and could kill another'. While only a few words, these were extremely important ones in the context of this enquiry. Unfortunately, due to family pressures, they would not make a written statement. While it was to be left unrecorded for the moment, it was never to be forgotten: 'The law has a long memory' (as Peter Taylor had earlier recounted).

Another of Russell's relations was interviewed by the police who told them about an occasion when Russell, Veronica and Samantha visited their house for a family meal. An argument occurred during dinner between Veronica and Russell during the visit and Veronica was shown to be wrong. Samantha told her relation that both she and her mother would have to do 'bow downs' which resemble the Moslem way of praying. This was a humiliating punishment dreamed up by Russell to maintain his dominance over his wife and daughter. This caused a row and resulted in the social gathering being terminated. Russell was asked to leave and he took his family with him. Veronica's relations found the humiliating treatment of her and Samantha to be quite disgusting.

CHAPTER 15

The Games Player:
Russell Causley Part Four

In the spring of 1996, John Major was leading the Conservative government to defeat, largely due to the public being sick of the corruption scandals in the party which brought about their downfall. This would see the advent the following year of an underrated, and largely unknown, young politician called Tony Blair, who would indelibly mark the next decade. Gary Glitter was about to be arrested and charged with downloading indecent images of children. The glitter began to fall off some of the pop celebrities who had become akin to royalty; and the Macpherson report on the police mishandling of the racist murder of Stephen Lawrence was released which damned them for just about everything.

Then that phone went again and a woman detective constable from the Devon and Cornwall Constabulary, Beverley Clapham, asked to speak to Detective Sergeant Stone.

'Do you know anything about a man called Russell Causley?' she asked. She was dealing with a series of frauds involving stolen motor vehicles and the main offender was Andrew Briggs, a career criminal specialising in fraud. He was in custody at HM Prison Exeter awaiting trial and was spending some time with Russell Causley who of course was awaiting trial for murder. DS Stone told her he knew a lot about Mr Causley! He sat back and listened intently.

Mr Briggs's wife had been implicated in some of his crimes and this had upset him as he did not want her to be prosecuted. He offered to tell the police about conversations between himself and Causley in the hope that he could help her. This was clearly not the best basis on which to start with a witness and I was very sceptical, but this is what we were presented with. Chris conferred with me and it was established that the officer dealing with him, Detective Constable Beverley Clapham, had no knowledge of this case and that is how she was asked to remain. We did, however, want to know what Mr Briggs had to say. This is his story: –

In early 1996 Briggs was sent to H.M. Prison Exeter to await trial for fraud. There he met Russell Causley and they associated and played chess together. They got to know each other by what was a time-honoured ritual of swapping stories about their criminal exploits, and what charges they were in prison for. Over some time and as their friendship grew, Russell Causley told Mr Briggs that two inmates had made statements implicating him in the murder of his wife. He completely dismissed one of these accounts but gave credence to the other. He told him he was initially going to shoot his wife by borrowing a gun from a friend who was a legitimate firearm certificate holder. However, events overtook him and during an argument she broke a pane of glass in the bathroom when she threw a stool at him, he lost control and killed her with a hatchet. With the help of two other people he took her to Burley in the New Forest. He said that he had dismembered her body which was weighted and put down a deep shaft. He told Mr Briggs that he took Samantha, his daughter, to London the next day having forged a note to himself from Veronica. He then went on to describe in some detail about an acquaintance of his called Archie who helped him dispose of the body, but who had not been present at the murder. He felt that Archie was weak and would confess everything to the police if caught. He said it was Archie's wife who impersonated Veronica by going into Bournemouth police station to report herself alive and well in 1985.

Mr Briggs elicited this information from Russell over a period of weeks and did not want to 'interrogate' Russell but made him amenable to talk about these things in a subtler way. He believed that Russell had only told him about his wife's murder because he wanted to start a homosexual relationship with him. Russell also talked at great length about his own sexual exploits which included bondage, particularly the use of handcuffs, and the dominant sexual treatment of Veronica of which she didn't approve. He also manipulated Veronica into having sex with Archie while Russell watched, again against her will. These descriptions made Mr Briggs quite sick at the thought of it and he tried to steer the conversations away from Russell's sexual fantasies. From time to time Russell would explode in rage, becoming manic and paced up and down in the cell. Mr Briggs described how Russell's eyes would almost pop out, as his face became distorted. At one-time Russell told him how he would dominate his wife and daughter by making them do 'bow downs' which he illustrated by imitating the Moslem prayer position.

The disclosures made by Mr Briggs could be corroborated by events which we knew to have taken place. For example, a friend of Russell's had already told us about a conversation he had had with him when he described a 'weekend from hell' having been involved in a prolonged argument with Veronica around the time of her disappearance. Another friend had told us how he had noticed broken glass in a bathroom door at Russell's house in Ipswich Road, again around the same time. Russell himself had admitted knowing Mr Lomond but denying any conversations about killing his wife, and he dismissed Mr Murphy completely. Subsequently the man Archie was never traced nor indeed did any of Russell's friends mention such a man. No dismembered body has ever been found as he described, in or around Burley in the New Forest, despite extensive searches carried out in that vicinity. The account of the killing was materially different from what Mr Murphy had said but did fall in line in part with the statement given by Mr Lomond. Russell had possession of his committal papers, which comprise statements and documents concerning the evidence against him, in his cell at HMP Exeter. Could Mr Briggs have had sight of them, could he remember so much, especially detail like the broken glass in the bathroom? Was he saying all this to get a lighter sentence for himself at his trial, and was he trying to get his own wife off the hook?

Briggs was a gift to the defence in that the account he would provide was vastly different from that given by the two earlier prisoner witnesses Lomond and Murphy. There were two possible options as to why Briggs had entered into this case. The first is that he wanted to protect his wife, to try to shield her from any possible charges relating to the criminal deceptions he was involved in. Secondly if he could curry favour with the police, he may have believed it possible to get a reduced sentence of imprisonment. His career as a fraudster was built on his ability to lie and cheat his way to getting innocent people to part with their money. On the other hand, it occurred to me that the disclosures by Mr Briggs came over six months after Mr Murphy had told the police about his conversations with Russell. We knew that Russell was an intelligent, cunning man who was already aware that two convicted criminals had reported to the police admissions he had made to them. Was he going to be stupid enough to keep broadcasting his guilt to all and sundry, criminals with whom he shared a cell, and provide the best directions yet to where he said he had hidden his wife's body? Or was it that Russell Causley, the chess player, who was playing a bigger game by feeding Briggs with false and deliberately misleading information, which would in turn cast doubt on the evidence given by Lomond and Murphy and throw the police off the scent? Russell Causley, the games player, was playing a game for his life and freedom. The CPS and counsel for the prosecution gave this matter great thought and finally it was decided not to use him as a prosecution witness, but offer him to the defence, who not unsurprisingly requested him to give evidence at the end of the prosecution case.

The summer of 1996 saw Chris and Paul fly off to Canada where they gathered evidence from Dorval Airport Montreal, Quebec, and Canadian Immigration Authorities, regarding the deportation in 1986 of Patricia Causley for impersonating Veronica. They also mopped up friends and acquaintances of Russell and his wife while there. One of these friends told Chris and Paul that they had only ever met two people in their life who they believed capable of murder. One of these was Kenneth Noye, a notorious British gangster, and the other was Russell Causley. The witness who they had unearthed was later to appear at Winchester Crown Court, and the evidence he gave had great impact on the court. Their whole visit to Canada was conducted with close support and assistance from the Royal Canadian Mounted Police. I made a similar trip to Germany, where I made enquiries in Berlin, Munich and Frankfurt, all places where Veronica and Russell had worked. I teamed up with a German policeman, Captain Horst Schmitt, who assisted me checking with all the official state record offices including driving licence and foreigner registration centres. During these enquiries, I also became accustomed to the German policeman's diet of white beer and sausages. I went on to establish Veronica's undoubted presence in Germany in 1978 and her total absence in that country thereafter.

During that summer, Chris and Paul executed a search warrant on a furniture storage facility in the Home Counties where they recovered *all* the suitcases belonging to Veronica and Russell, plus a much-prized vanity set which Samantha told us was her mother's favourite possession. Importantly they came across a tape on which Chris and Paul's visit to Russell and Patricia at Cooks Broom in June 1994 had been recorded. It was a virtually verbatim account of the conversation they had written into their pocket book two years earlier.

During the summer, as well as excavations in the New Forest, we called in assistance from Doctor Margaret Cox, a forensic archaeologist at Bournemouth University. She carried out an archaeological examination at Russell's house in Ipswich Road. She and her team examined the foundations underneath the floor boards and she was confident there had been no disturbance of the earth nor was a body buried at that site. The house was of the older type, with suspended joists between the foundation walls, rather than a concrete base as in modern construction methods. Her team carried out exhaustive examinations of graveyards in Bournemouth, with particular attention to newly dug graves, but again found nothing. The techniques used by Doctor Cox enabled her to carry out these searches in a very thorough manner with the minimum disruption at the different sites. Samantha had told us that the garage of the property had an inspection pit which her father had concreted over. Once again, we dug that up, and once again, we found nothing.

As with any major enquiry, we had our twists and turns, ups and downs and probably more in this case than most. Mr Lomond decided to complicate things by absconding from an open prison where he was completing his sentence. He went on the run because boiling water mixed with sugar had been poured down his back. It had been discovered by his fellow inmates that he had made a statement to the police. This in their world amounted to being a 'grass'. To make things even worse than the disappearance of our prime witness was that as the date for the trial approached, he went to Dorchester, the county town of Dorset, and carried out a fraud. After a little while on the run, and with Chris and Paul on his tail, (the local police near his home didn't see the capture of a fraudster on the run as a big priority), Lomond was arrested. He was taken back to Dorchester and interviewed about the bank fraud he committed there. Dorchester was at this time a different police division with its own command structure from Bournemouth. What the police in Dorchester decided to do with him was a matter for them. Personally, I hoped they would charge him, which in turn would prolong his sentence and mean it would be easy for me to produce him from prison as a serving prisoner rather than have to trust him to attend if he were at liberty. Not very nice of me I know, but I needed this witness to testify in a murder case and producing him from prison could be guaranteed but relying on him to turn up with no benefit to himself was a much riskier proposition. While my hand hovered over the phone, I dared not interfere. As it turned out the police at Dorchester decided not to charge him. They considered – understandably – that as he had only served one year of a three-year sentence; and had absconded from prison for which he would be sanctioned, he would be unlikely to get any longer sentence than the one he was already serving, and a further trial would be a waste of the court's time and public money. This was a decision which would come back to haunt me as 'human rights' lawyers would later place a different and darker reason on this course of action.

Between 8 and 18 December 1996 Russell Causley stood trial for murder at Winchester Crown Court. Samantha gave evidence and felt better for doing so, friends and acquaintances of Russell's came from all over the world to testify, as did Mr Lomond and Mr Murphy. In fact, both men had completed their sentences and were free men when they gave their evidence. Despite my doubts and cynicism, they both attended willingly and came from different parts of the country under their own steam. After they had finished giving their evidence, I thanked them both profusely; neither man at any stage ever asked for payment, or favour of any kind; nor was any given.

Captain Horst Schmitt came to Winchester from Munich. The defence 'dropped it on our toes' during the trial that they required him to give evidence in person, having had his statement for months. He was flown to court overnight and appeared the next day. He told the court what we knew, that Veronica had not been in Germany since 1978 and was not there now. No unidentified bodies of females matching her distinctive description (through operation scars) remained unidentified. Lieutenant Riette Le Blanc RCMP from Quebec was called the evening before she was required to give evidence, once again a last-minute demand by the defence. She flew over that night and landed at Heathrow at 7.15 am. By 10.30 am that day she was in the witness box at Winchester giving evidence. Luckily, the last-minute scramble and the determination of a German and Canadian police officer matched the determination of their soul-mates in Britain.

The defence also threw down a challenge in that they wanted to hear from Mr Briggs. We produced him to the court from Exeter prison where he was serving his sentence for the fraud for which he had been arrested. I personally warned him in no uncertain terms before he gave evidence of the importance of telling the truth and the serious consequences of perverting the course of justice, a major crime for which imprisonment is almost a complete certainty. I told him I would personally nail him to the floor if he was lying. He implored me that what he had told us was absolutely 'God's honest truth' and that he had nothing to gain by lying as he had already been sentenced. Once my sermon to him was over he was whisked off from the police cells at Bournemouth to Winchester Crown Court. He gave impeccable evidence, stuck like glue to what he had said in his written statement and created a positive impression all round.

I found myself in the witness box towards the end of the trial and answered questions regarding our dealings with Mr Lomond and Mr Murphy. I made it clear that they were not offered any inducements to make their statements. I also told the court that Mr Briggs had not received any favours and in particular a 'text' in reward for him giving evidence when he was sentenced. A text is a letter to the judge, setting out how helpful a defendant has been in assisting the police. The judge may give a discount on a sentence in light of such a letter, so it is important that the jury knows that the information has not been given to achieve this. Chris and Paul gave evidence, much of which was accepted by the defence and in particular the accuracy of their conversation with Russell at Cooks Broom in June 1994. 163 statements had been taken and over 850 separate actions carried out largely by two, then four CID officers. The trial lasted two weeks and on 18 December 1996 after barely two hours the jury returned a unanimous verdict of guilty to murder. Whilst a police officer is supposed to be dispassionate and emotionless, it was once again that old feeling akin to scoring the winning goal for England. This was all done with a straight face, and serious countenance. An Appeal concerning alleged inadequate warnings given by the trial judge in respect of the evidence given by the three convicted criminals was later dismissed by the Appeal Court. Once again it is important to remember that it is not only the police who are involved in bringing criminals to justice. The whole case would never have entered the judicial system if John Revell, the head of the CPS in Bournemouth, had not had the courage to take a risk and bring charges in the first place. The barrister he had conferred with before those charges were brought was Anthony Donne QC, a highly skilled lawyer and wordsmith. He went on from his early advice to conduct a prosecution so skilful that not one of the twelve jurors doubted Causley's guilt.

Sometime later, Chris and I went to visit Russell in prison to ask him to at last tell us the truth and disclose the whereabouts of the body of his wife. As he walked down the corridor of the prison, he spotted us some way off. He said to his warder, 'I don't want to see them.' He spun on his heel and walked away. We had no power, not even in prison, to question him if he did not want to see us. That was it, a satisfactory conclusion at the trial but again disappointment at being unable to set to rest properly the body of a murdered wife and mother.

CHAPTER 16

Cruising

Hampstead Heath is at the northern edge of E Division in the Metropolitan Police District. In early 1971 together with a bunch of recruits, a bunch of pretty naive rookies at that, I was shown around the Division by a long-in-the-tooth sergeant. We visited this expanse of parkland surrounded by its fashionable and very expensive houses as part of our familiarisation. Under the veneer of respectability and sedate gardens there lurked a darker world. The sergeant told us, that we should be alive to the fact that at night, certain areas of the heath were taken over by 'poofters'. This was the language of the time; the word 'gay' had not yet entered the lexicon. He elaborated his knowledge by describing that they tended to dress in white polo-necked jumpers and engaged in a variety of sexual acts with other men. Open sex in a public place is an offence and officers were trained to arrest and prosecute anyone caught committing such acts. However, as the sergeant finished his colourful accounts of various activities uncovered, he gave us this warning: Should any of these homosexual men complain of being beaten-up for sport – known at the time as 'queer bashing'- then we should take such a complaint extremely seriously. He emphasised that the next bashing up of a homosexual could lead to a murder and he quoted several such cases that he had been involved in investigating.

Unfortunately, at this time, most policemen, and indeed broader society used the words 'queer' and 'poofter' to describe homosexual men. Whilst I never felt these descriptions were homophobic or hateful, they were definitely demeaning. The result is that a whole section of society was stigmatised and felt alienated from the police. This in turn led them to believing that the police would take little notice of any complaint they made, for fear of being arrested or vilified and therefore led to an under-reporting of any assaults or crimes committed against them. The wise words of the sergeant never left me and I, like my colleagues, were very watchful for any signs of this type of incident.

On 5 July 1995 at a little after 1 am I was aroused from a deep sleep by the force control room. I was told that the body of a man had been found in Boscombe Chine Gardens, an area of extensive parkland stretching from the main road between Boscombe and Bournemouth and leading to the cliffs overlooking Bournemouth beach. The gardens which were created in the late Victorian era covered an area of several acres and were wooded with winding paths and clearings dotted with ornate beds of flowers and shrubbery. I was told by the control room sergeant that Detective Superintendent Steve Maidment from police headquarters was on the way and he had asked for me to meet him at the scene. Steve and I had served as detective sergeants at Boscombe together. He was ruggedly handsome, highly intelligent, possessed a quick wit and was probably the best detective I have ever known.

I drove along Christchurch Road, past some decaying houses and saw in the street lights a uniformed constable by the entrance to Boscombe Chine Gardens. He was setting up a roll of tape with the words 'police line, do not cross' written on it. The officer recognised me and directed me to follow the main path into the gardens to a shelter in the centre of this large park, which was about fifty yards or so from the entrance. I made my way along the winding path towards a torch light I could see in the distance. As I approached, I could see the shape of a uniformed police inspector who was wielding a bright lantern. It was Pete Mole, an unflappable, solid officer who was in charge of the Division that night. We exchanged brief salutations and Pete directed me to a garden bench near the centre of the gardens where a number of paths intersected. I could just make out the shape of a man lying on his side near the bench.

As I approached, I saw dimly on the tarmac path what looked like flint chippings, some ten to fifteen feet from the body. They glistened in the torch light and as I studied them, I realised that they were in fact fragments of his skull. The body was that of a young man, dressed in a track suit, lying on the ground between a bench and a waste bin. He was lying on his left side and I noticed that he had extensive head injuries. I saw on the bench a chrome cigarette or tobacco case; the lid was flipped open and it glinted when the torch light struck it. I didn't approach any further; he was obviously dead and this was clearly a murder. It is of paramount importance that the scene of a crime be preserved and unnecessary walking around and poking about must be avoided as it will destroy forensic evidence, some of which can be tiny. Meticulous forensic examination was later carried out and shards of the man's skull were found fifteen feet away in one direction from his body and ten feet away in another. I looked about from the scene where the body lay. The nearest lights I could see were from houses and flats about a hundred yards away. Where we stood was pitch black, there was no moon and I remember thinking, where the hell are we going to start with this one? Steve arrived within minutes and after he had assessed the scene, we made our way back to the main entrance to the gardens, both in a somewhat pensive mood with what lay before us.

The body was that of Paul Bradshaw, a single man who lived nearby. Both Steve and I had clearly defined roles, I was the crime manager for the Division and my job was to set up a major incident room and find all the staffing. Steve was the operational detective superintendent and busied himself with investigating the case. The first place to start was with whoever found the body and establish how that had come about.

I then dived into the well-established procedures of calling in the specialist HOLMES team from police headquarters; contacting the house to house uniform sergeant who would come in and prepare the area to be subject to intense visits by teams of uniformed constables; and last, but not least, gather the detectives required to make the enquiries. I called in Detective Inspector Watts, a suave and meticulous detective with an outstanding track record, which included the conviction of a child murderer several years earlier, in which he was instrumental. We agreed the rough number of officers required and he immediately got to grips with the high priority enquiries regarding the discovery of the body. This was a cold start murder; there was no obvious suspect, the motive was unknown and this would be one of the first issues to establish. A lone man on his own in a park after midnight could have been murdered for many reasons: perhaps an assault by someone known to him; a gang-related killing; a robbery or many other motives. Most of the staff would come from the Bournemouth Division, but assistance would be needed from neighbouring police stations and once again I was back fighting with the usual suspects, the local Divisional commanders, to release their officers to this enquiry.

While I was running about trying to set up all this staffing and logistics, Steve was getting on with the job of what, where, when, why, how and who. It was soon established that the body of Paul Bradshaw had been found by two men, Colin Wake and David Johnson, who had been returning to their flat from a house party in Southbourne a mile or so to the east of Boscombe Chine Gardens. Their flat was in a block just to the west of the gardens which it overlooked, so their explanation seemed reasonable. However, when I read their statements, I remember they explained that they took about an hour to walk home. I knew the area well, it was my patch and the journey should have taken half that time. Something wasn't right. They explained that when they were crossing Boscombe Chine Gardens towards their flat, they found the body of Paul Bradshaw lying on the ground. They noticed a large amount of blood around him, panicked and ran off to find help. They immediately ran towards Christchurch Road and flagged down a passing taxi and told the driver what they had found and to call the police, they were both in an agitated and excitable state. Paul 'Snapper' Duncan, a quiet, dry-witted detective constable with an infectious grin was one of those officers who spoke to the two men who had found the body. He was instinctively not happy with what these men said, or how they said it. The trousers worn by Wake were bloodstained, but not his top clothing.

The detectives who interviewed the two men communicated their misgivings to Steve Maidment who accepted their judgement and agreed with their reservations. The intuition, opinions and experience from detectives rich in experience, but junior in rank, are given great weight by their senior commanders. With the concerns of the detectives around the timings of when they left the party to the discovery of the body, as well as the presence of the blood stains; Steve decided that whilst the two men were not suspects, the evidence of the blood stains on their clothing should be preserved. These items could then be forensically examined to ascertain the pattern and type of blood stains and not least to establish whose blood it was. There was insufficient evidence to arrest the men; they had, after all, just found his body and immediately run for assistance. A witness statement was taken from them, there and then, as to what they had seen and done. They were taken home after their statements were completed and with their consent, a cursory search was made of their flat, but nothing of significance was found inside. However, a pair of bloodstained jeans were found just outside their flat which David Johnson said were his and he explained that the blood on them was from when he had recently cut his arm. This was later found to be the case.

Later that morning, at 11.15, Steve Maidment attended Boscombe mortuary where a full autopsy was carried out on the body of Paul Bradshaw. The Home Office pathologist was Doctor Allen Anscombe. It was established that death was due to multiple blows to the head; at least seven in the opinion of the pathologist. These were some of the worst head injuries this highly experienced pathologist had ever witnessed. On the back of the deceased could be seen a straight line with several indentation marks at one end; it gave the appearance of a club with studs at one end. The investigators now knew that this was likely to be some kind of weapon, the injuries had been deliberately inflicted and with great severity. The injuries inflicted to the back were also clear evidence that these were not defensive wounds but inflicted from behind; about as good evidence of murder as you can get. The question, though, was why and by whom?

Paul Bradshaw was not a local man but had come to Bournemouth from London where he had worked in a casino and in the hotel trade. He had also travelled extensively and had lived and worked in east and South Africa. He was a single man, living alone near the hotel on East Overcliff where he worked as a barman. He was described by his employer as a quiet, pleasant man, but a bit of a loner. He had been the victim of a vicious robbery some four years earlier, but the attacker was never caught.

The clothing worn by the two men who found the body was sent to the forensic science laboratory where it was examined by a scientist whose area of expertise was blood stains. It was quickly established that the blood found on the clothing came from Paul Bradshaw, the victim. The pattern and nature of the blood stains were then analysed by the scientist who told Steve verbally that the pattern and shape of the blood stains recovered indicated to him that the two men must have been stood close to the victim when the blows were inflicted. This information was initially passed to the incident room by a phone call.

With the pretty solid forensic evidence to hand, albeit verbally, and with the elasticated timing between when Wake and Johnson left the party in Southbourne and finding the body, Steve instructed that the two men be arrested on suspicion of murder and questioned in the light of the evidence uncovered so far. On 13 July 1995, the men were arrested in their flat at 36, Manor Road and taken to Bournemouth police station where they were interviewed. The flat and grounds were searched for any article which may have made the injuries to Mr Bradshaw's head and back – nothing was found. They vehemently denied being responsible for the killing of Mr Bradshaw and explained that the blood must have got onto them because they turned his body over to see if he was still alive. This they adamantly maintained was how the blood stains must have splashed onto them. DI Geoff Watts and Snapper Duncan who interviewed them did not accept their explanations, but the only person who could refute these claims by the dispassionate use of forensic science was the scientist himself, who had clearly said that 'they must have been close to the victim when the blows were inflicted.'

The written statement of the scientist containing the definitive words he would utter from the witness box became crucial. Steve would not authorise a charge until he had got his hands on the black and white signed statement from the scientist to this effect. When it finally arrived, Steve was shocked to his core. The scientist stated that despite his initial belief, he could not refute the possibility that the stains on the clothing may have got there when the suspects turned the body over. Steve was livid, the air turned blue and this highly professional detective exploded in righteous indignation which he still remembers to this day. The case, which was already difficult, was going nowhere. The suspects had denied everything; there was no weapon recovered; there was no independent witnesses and the blood stains were not conclusive. The suspects were released.

The next day, 14 July, the body of a young man was found hanging from a tree in Boscombe Chine Gardens. Steve called into my office and we both went back again to the scene of the earlier murder. This part of Boscombe Gardens comprised a chine, or a small valley which leads towards the sea just off Christchurch Road. While there were already suspects in this case it could not be ruled out that another person was responsible for the murder; such must be the thinking of the SIO. It was possible that we could find a suicide note on the dead man confessing to the murder and revealing where the weapon was hidden. However, nothing was found, either in his pockets or in his bedsit where he had lived nearby. As the fire brigade, gently and with great care lowered his body to the ground Steve said, 'Probably some poor nutter who nobody gives a damn about.'

The enquiry then settled down into a rhythm which is typical of long-running detailed investigations where suspects are known, but no stone is left unturned, in-case indeed, the prime suspects are innocent and the real killer has evaded detection. Boscombe Chine Gardens was a magnet after dark for homosexual men, often those who were closet homosexuals, or just wanted a casual sexual experience. A major thrust of the investigation was to trace any person who may have been in the gardens that evening leading up to the time of the discovery of the body – and there were quite a few. Several people came forward, some reluctantly, to give their accounts of passing through the gardens that evening and recount what or who they saw. These were the brave ones, but the majority hung back, many were afraid they would be arrested and or vilified by the police for their actions. This resulted in a lot of sightings of 'man in red tee shirt with man in yellow tee shirt' and so on, but being unable to identify them, potential witnesses were being lost. A large list was compiled of unknown people, largely men who needed to be traced, implicated or eliminated in the murder; each one may have been a crucial witness or a suspect. Trying to find these people was not going to be easy.

It was therefore imperative for the police to gain the confidence of the local gay community if they wanted to catch the killer or killers and prevent further recurrence of a crime of this extreme violence. The leading light in breaking into this, up to then, close community, came in the form of Steve Pugh, a handsome, charismatic policeman, heterosexual, very charming and with the ability to disarm and set at ease almost anybody.

Steve was a uniformed constable who was employed as the home beat officer, or local community beat officer, for the Crescent area of Boscombe. This was one of the more run-down parts of Boscombe which adjoined the very affluent area of Bournemouth overcliff, which is populated with expensive houses and hotels; and which is separated in part and abuts against Boscombe Chine Gardens. Steve, as a good community beat officer, knew most of the residents, good and bad, who lived in this area. Very importantly, he had good contacts with members of the local gay community, largely because many of them worked in Bournemouth's hotel and hospitality sector. He had also taken reports of crime from some gay men and had demonstrated his integrity by dealing with them without prejudice, ridicule or disrespect – he demonstrated that he was a man who could be trusted. With this knowledge in mind, and knowing he had a lot to offer the enquiry, which was struggling because it had no links to the group of people it needed to, Steve Pugh made direct contact with the SIO. Steve Maidment didn't need asking twice and absorbed this energetic community beat constable onto the investigation and made him something the Dorset Police had never before done, he became the Lesbian and Gay Police Liaison Officer along with Sandy Robertson, that caring Family Liaison Officer from the Du Rose case.

Steve and Sandy, using the contacts he had established, soon started getting underneath the surface of the cruising scene, as it was called, in Boscombe Gardens. They were put in touch with a biker who used the moniker Big Bear, who came from a group with the nickname 'the bears' because they were well built physically with long hair and bushy beards. This man opened the lid on the underground culture, told them all about different groups who frequent the area, from the 'chickens' so called because they tended to be young men, to the older casual sex seekers called the 'hens', who hung about in an area colloquially known as the elephants' graveyard. The various territories where different groups mingled were pointed out, but the identity of those involved was not. Big Bear was suspicious about Steve and Sandy and feared that after this investigation was concluded the police would be back to hound his friends. He asked, 'Can you assure me that anything I give you will not be used against us?' Steve, using that discretion given to a constable said, 'Yes,' and he stuck to his promise like glue, confirming the confidence the gay community had shown in him and underlining his integrity.

Many of the men who loiter near public toilets or known pick up spots for homosexuals are often those men who are not openly gay, but often lead a double life, being married to a woman and having children. They do not usually frequent the gay scene, pubs and clubs where everyone is open about their sexuality but keep it secret. These are the very hard to reach groups.

Over the next four to five months Steve and Sandy visited every gay club or pub in Bournemouth and surrounding area. They spoke to hundreds of gay men and managed to identify and eliminate a number of men who had been in the area of the gardens on the night of the murder. Furthermore, they followed up every report of robbery committed on males within a ten-mile radius of the gardens. Steve Maidment wanted to double check every complaint of street robbery, just in case the victims may not have wanted the police to know that actually they may have been loitering about in a public place to engage in sexual acts with other men – they were worried about being arrested. I remember distinctly and to my shame, that about a week before the murder of Paul Bradshaw, I was reading through the daily list of crimes for the Bournemouth area, as was one of my duties each day. This daily crime state usually contained all crimes, usually about fifty, committed during the last twenty-four hours in Bournemouth. I noticed one reported crime was a street robbery on a lone male in Sea Road, Boscombe, which is about half a mile from the gardens. I remember at the time thinking it was a bit unusual as the location was very public and that type of crime was out of character with the area. I made sure it was being overlooked by a detective and passed on to myriad other problems that day. Robbery is a word often misused to describe the theft of property, it is in fact much more; robbery is an offence of theft but coupled with it is the threat of or use of violence, it carries a sentence of life imprisonment and is therefore high on a detective's priority list.

Steve Pugh and Sandy Robertson re-interviewed the victim in this case, one Arson Barbour and he admitted that the robbery had taken place in Boscombe Gardens and not Sea Road as he had reported. He had been nervous about admitting that he had been in Boscombe Gardens because he wanted to keep his night time activities secret and he thought the police might arrest him. However, with the disarming nature of Steve and Sandy he revealed the truth and made a fresh statement. He went onto give descriptions of the two men who robbed him which were very similar to Wake and Johnson. As a result of this fresh evidence they were arrested for robbery on Mr Barbour and placed on an identity parade. Wake was identified as being one of those responsible for the robbery and charged with this crime. Johnson was not identified and released.

The location given by Mr Barbour as to where in the gardens this had happened, the time and the threats made, as well as weapons brandished by the assailants, was very similar to the modus operandi of the killers of Mr Bradshaw. The position of Mr Bradshaw's cigarette tin on the body when it was discovered could have been as a result of the killers rifling the body to steal valuables, something that occurred to me as a possible motive when I first attended the scene. The robbery of Mr Barbour would have been good supporting evidence had Wake been charged with murder, but there was just not enough evidence to bring this further charge, even with the blood pattern stains.

The trial for the robbery took place at the crown court some months later. However, during the trial his girl- friend, Susan Stamp, claimed that they were together at the time of the crime and he was nowhere near Boscombe Chine Gardens. The jury believed her and Wake was acquitted of the robbery and released – a free man once again.

Things were not going well for the small investigation team; the forensic evidence initially thought strong was inconclusive; Wake's involvement in a robbery with strikingly similar characteristics to the murder failed to result in a conviction and people close to the suspects were keeping their lips sealed. One person who had been on the periphery of the two men was a family relative known as A.J. Bennett. Steve and his team were never fully happy with what he had said when he had provided an alibi for both Wake and Johnson by saying that they had all been at a party together in Southbourne and he saw them leave together just before they told police they had stumbled across the body. However, other people at the same party reported Wake and Johnson leaving earlier, but those witnesses could not be certain, if called upon to swear in court to exactly what time they had left. The police were not convinced by Bennett's account of events and tried to trace him again and interview him in more detail. However, when they went to his address in Bournemouth, he was missing. Not to be defeated, they contacted all his known friends and relatives and managed to discover that he had left England for South Africa. Enquiries were made in South Africa by the murder and robbery squad and he was traced to Durban.

On 11 April 1996 and after some battles with sceptical senior officers at headquarters who needed convincing that this was a legitimate line of enquiry, Steve Maidment and his deputy Detective Inspector Geoff Watts flew out to South Africa to speak to this potentially crucial witness. There are strict protocols about police officers interviewing residents in a foreign country and the South African police insisted that they would collect Mr Bennett from where he was staying and bring him into the police station for the British police to interview. They would remain throughout and stay firmly in charge of all such procedures. Steve was apprehensive about this because the South African police had a somewhat suspect reputation due to their interrogation techniques on black Africans during the apartheid era.

However, those concerns were quickly put to rest when Mr Bennett arrived, having been treated with professionalism. He quickly admitted to Steve and Geoff that he had let loyalty to a family member get the better of him and had been troubled by his conscience. He revealed to the two senior detectives that Johnson and Wake had returned earlier to their flat at 36, Manor Road on the night of the murder from the party in Southbourne. He also told them that several days previously, they told him that a friend of theirs had been beaten up and they wanted to teach the attacker a lesson. They knew that he had a pick axe handle studded with screws at one end, which he explained he had made himself because he feared being attacked by some men who had been making threats against him. Mr Bennett went to his flat nearby and returned with the weapon which he gave to Wake and Johnson. Shortly after this the two men left the flat with the pick axe handle which he never saw again, – it was never found. The fact that Mr Bennett had supplied them with what would become a murder weapon and that he was aware that it could be used to assault someone may have been a factor in his earlier un-willingness to be more cooperative with the police. With a written statement from this crucial witness the two detectives returned to Dorset and this long tortuous enquiry received a boost of rocket fuel.

Snapper was tasked with liaising with Mr Bennett and trying to reconstruct an exact replica of the murder weapon. Mr Bennett was a builder and had acquired a pick axe handle and sixteen hexagonal head screws from a builders' merchants in Wiltshire, with which he made the club; he still had some screws from the same batch he had made the weapon with. Snapper visited the same builders' merchants and purchased the identical material. This was sent to the forensic science laboratory where a duplicate club was constructed. It was later tested on the carcass of a pig and an identical pattern of injury was reproduced when it was compared with the photograph of injuries to the back of Mr Bradshaw.

A case was then presented to the CPS that with the suspects now being squarely within the time frame and location of the murder, with the weapon used being reconstructed from the marks on the body of Mr Bradshaw and the crucial evidence from Mr Bennett putting the murder weapon in the hands of the two prime suspects and additionally the forensic evidence of the blood stains on their clothing, application was made to charge the suspects with murder. The result of this additional evidence, as well as our knowledge that prosecution cases grow as the case unfolds in the crown court, expectations were high. However, the CPS came back with the resounding decision that there was still not enough evidence to charge! The CPS must make a judgement that the prosecution case must have a realistic prospect of a conviction. In criminal cases this means that the evidence presented to the jury will lead them to decide that the defendant is guilty 'beyond reasonable doubt.' This means that the jury must be so sure that a person is guilty as to be certain, it is – rightly – an extremely high bar.

The whole enquiry team were plunged into a state of depression; they had moved mountains in this long running investigation to a point where the police would have charged the suspects had that power not have been taken away some years earlier. A lot of soul searching went on. Where did we go wrong? What have we missed? What more can we do? It was a sad day for all, not least Mr Bradshaw's relatives and the enquiry was closed down.

CHAPTER 17

The Unravelling

In the summer of 1997, Lynne Rachael Doughty contacted the police in Bournemouth following a drunken domestic incident at a house in Kinson, Bournemouth, present at which was Colin Wake and his girlfriend, Susan Stamp. The police attended what was a routine incident of disorder and after the situation was found to be passive, no further police action was deemed necessary. The uniformed constables who attended the incident were aware that Wake was suspected of murder and felt that this minor incident, no matter how small, may be of interest to the CID team. Such close working relations are essential and Snapper, being based at Bournemouth, was informed.

He with another detective who had worked on the case, set off to dig into the matter and find out what this was all about. They traced Lynne Doughty, who they established was a niece of Susan Stamp, the partner of Colin Wake, and the alibi witness in the robbery case. They took some time to establish a rapport with her having detected that she was taut and anxious about something. After gentle probing she told the officers that one evening, in the November following the murder, that she, Johnson and his then girlfriend Susan Stamp, all returned home, merry from a night out. Wake was particularly talkative and seemed to ramble on for some time before bursting into tears and confessed to the killing of Paul Bradshaw. He said in an emotional state. 'I beat him so severely in the head with a bat that his brains were scattered all over the gardens.' Miss Doughty pressed Wake on this and he then added in an excitable state, 'But I enjoyed it because he was gay and I hate butty men.' He then went onto describe how he and Johnson lied to the police about the finding of the body and how they had flagged down a taxi asking for help. Miss Doughty then said that Wake went up to bed and his girl-friend followed shortly after. She was very shaken up by all this, was the worse for wear with drink, didn't go home because she was un-fit to drive and stayed awake, dazed and confused all night. She explained that this knowledge troubled her deeply and she couldn't keep it bottled up inside her any longer. The officers took a long written statement from her detailing all this conversation, which was a very brave thing for her to do.

The case of robbery on Mr Barbour by Wake was also re-investigated and the false alibi was uncovered and he was charged with perverting the course of justice. This offence he was later to admit.

In August 1997, Wake and Johnson were arrested for a second time for the murder and questioned regarding their involvement in it. Detective Inspector Watts, an accomplished interviewer, questioned the men about their involvement which they both denied, sticking to their rickety stories. During the interview of Wake, DI Watts put all the salient points to him one after another, heaping up a case so convincingly that Wake must have realised the game was up. There was a long agonising pause, the silence became deafening. Just at the point, DI Watts believes, that Wake was going to admit the murder, his legal representative interjected that the DI's summary was nothing but a hypothesis. Wake pulled back from the brink and never again came close to admitting the crime. DI Watts has never forgotten that this interruption was made at such a critical point and to intentionally disrupt the rhythm of the interview. However, despite the denials, the CPS at last had a copper-bottomed case with the statement of Miss Doughty and approved the charging of both suspects with murder. This was the last day of service in the Dorset Police for Detective Superintendent Maidment. It could have not been a finer end to such a distinguished career. Geoff Watts, his deputy, made sure that a special delivery reached him before he left police headquarters: a copy of the *Daily Echo* carrying the story and a pack of South African beer.

The trial of the two men took place at Winchester Crown Court in October 1998. At the outset, Wake pleaded guilty to perverting the course of justice in relation to the robbery of Mr Barbour, but both men pleaded not guilty to murder.

Fortunately, the judge allowed the jury in the murder trial to hear about the robbery of Mr Barbour which had taken place a week before the killing, despite the best efforts of the defence to keep this evidence from being put to the jury. Evidence was heard from Mr Bennett about his construction of the weapon and the matching of the screws recovered by Snapper to the marks on the body. More forensic evidence was heard from the scientist in relation to the blood spattering on the defendants' clothes and a detailed account given by the pathologist in relation to the severity of the wounds – which were some of the worst he had ever seen. Miss Doughty gave evidence about the tearful account Wake had given of his killing of Mr Bradshaw and the appalling account of how his brains were scattered all over the gardens; in corroboration of what I had noticed at the scene when I attended two years earlier.

And then the trial took a quite unexpected turn and the defendants turned on each other. David Johnson went into the witness box and blamed Colin Wake for the killing. He told the court that at the time of the murder he had been drinking twelve cans of beer a day and taking amphetamines, cannabis and barbiturates. He had initially told the police the same lies as Wake to cover up the killing. He described how he and Wake returned to their flat at 36, Manor Road having been to a party in Southbourne. He said that in the flat was an axe handle with screws in it at one end which he had taken from a friend the previous night. He said that the weapon just cropped up in conversation which Wake began swinging around in the flat. Wake then said that he was going to try it out and disappeared outside. Johnson thought he meant he was going to hit a fence or a tree with it. But as he saw Wake walk to the end of the drive, he started to get worried. He said, 'One half of me thought he was messing about and he was going to go down the path and pretend, but when he didn't come back I was very worried. About a minute later I heard four or five thudding sounds like a person being hit with the club and twenty-five seconds after that I saw him walking up the path.' He then said that they went back into the flat and decided to see how badly hurt the person was who he had just hit. Johnson told the court that he and Wake told the police they had found the body he said, 'I didn't tell the full story because I was scared the police may have misinterpreted my involvement and I was worried for my own personal safety.'

Guy Boney QC, defending Wake, in cross examination, told the court that Johnson owed up to £1,000 to drug dealers and that it was Johnson who had taken the weapon to Boscombe gardens to rob gay men who illicitly used the gardens that night. This was put to Johnson which he denied. Mr Boney said, 'I suggest you came across Mr Bradshaw on your own and attacked him. Wake had followed you into the gardens and shouted from a few yards away, "Dave, Dave". He then ran up to you while you were still beating Bradshaw's head and he actually pulled the club from your hand.' Again, this was denied.

Paul Chad, counsel for the prosecution, said to Johnson, 'You both told the same story to police afterwards, because the truth is that you are both in it together, you are cutting your own throats in the hope of escaping responsibility for what you have done to this unfortunate creature.'

Colin Wake then told the jury that it was Johnson's idea to go to the park to rob someone, but he refused. He said Johnson became angry, because he had earlier refused to lend him some money. He followed after Johnson, who had the pick axe handle and when still some distance away heard a thud and saw two shadowy figures. He then ran forward and grabbed the club from Johnson's hand. He then described how they both returned to their nearby flat and Johnson changed his clothes because they were bloodstained. They both then went back to the gardens where he claimed that he saw how much blood there was and ran to phone for an ambulance. He admitted he told the police that they had stumbled across the body whilst walking through the park. It was put to him that he hated gays, but he denied this. He said that he had known David Johnson since their school days but had fallen out with him since he found out that he was going to tell the 'truth'.

Mr Chad, in cross-examination, said that they had acted together and were both in the park with a fearsome weapon with the intention of carrying out a homophobic attack on a gay person. This was again denied.

So, with the end of the evidence from the prosecution and defence and after the closing speeches by both counsel and guidance from the judge, the jury retired to consider their verdicts. While there was direct evidence from both defendants, this was not necessarily as good as it looked from the police point of view. The question the jury had to consider was, who killed Mr Bradshaw? Was it Wake? Was it Johnson? Or was it both of them together in what in law is called 'joint enterprise'? This is where two or more people join in committing a single crime, in circumstances where they are, in effect, all joint principals. This includes a situation where one of those involved may actually do or carry out more physical action than the other, but they are both equally committed to doing the act. If the jury considered beyond all reasonable doubt that this was the case, then they could return a verdict of guilty to both Wake and Johnson, whoever wielded the pick axe handle. On the other hand, they could have convicted one of murder if they thought that only one of them intended to commit the crime if the other had no control over their actions or tried to stop them. The worst possible outcome, and it has happened many times, would be for the jury to acquit both, because they did not know who caused the fatal blows and they did not accept that it was a joint enterprise.

There was a tense wait by all those officers who had worked so hard to establish the truth in this case. Finally, after some hours of deliberation the jury returned with a unanimous verdict of guilty of murder by both men. The trial judge, Lord Justice John Kay, said when sentencing them both to life imprisonment, 'It was quite a dreadful murder, because you both took the nastiest weapon I've ever come across and beat that man in the most violent manner. It was for no other reason than he was homosexual and you deliberately picked on him and killed him.' Wake was given a concurrent term of five years imprisonment for perverting the course of justice.

On 15 May 2008, the minimum term to be served by Wake and Johnson was considered in the High Court of Justice, Queens Bench Division. The deliberation by that court is interesting because it throws light on the considerations by the judge at the original trial. The facts of the case were again considered and took account of the admissions that the defendants had changed some bloodstained clothes, and then returned to the scene of the murder by a different route before they raised the alarm. The trial judge was satisfied that Wake had struck the fatal blows and equally satisfied that it was Johnson's idea and he had provided the weapon. He found it was impossible to distinguish between their culpability. The trial judge also considered that in relation to the robbery that Wake and his girlfriend had advanced a false alibi and that Johnson had been a party to the robbery, but there was no evidence other than Wake's assertion. Johnson struck the trial judge as intelligent and calculating and detected that he had no hint of sympathy for Mr Bradshaw, or any realisation that other people would disapprove of such criminal activity as he was prepared to admit to. In relation to Miss Doughty, the niece of Wake's girlfriend, he found her to be an impressive and compelling witness. The court set a minimum term of imprisonment for these killers at fifteen years and nine months before being considered for release on licence by the parole board.

The murder of Mr Bradshaw was carried out with such extreme violence – seven blows to the head, with skull fragments scattered in every direction for up to fifteen feet – and can only be described as one of barbaric evil. However, the police did not give up on the hunt for the killers and were determined, within the investigation team, to bring the perpetrators to justice. This alone was not enough; A.J. Bennett, a blood relative to one of the defendants, and Lynne Doughty a niece of the other offender's girlfriend, were caught in a difficult place. They had loyalty to friends and family and felt they could not disclose what they had seen or heard. Loyalty is important; it is one of our early survival tools. By its very nature we need to stick together as groups to hunt, defend our tribe and maintain social cohesion. On the other hand, there are times when loyalty to others, whether friends or families, can become misplaced and is superseded by the morals and interests of larger society – this was easily one such case. Miss Doughty had to wrestle with her conscience and brave the possible threats from the perpetrators and their friends and other self-appointed moral judges, such as those who would call her a 'grass'. It took a great deal of courage to stand up for justice, but this very ordinary lady did an extraordinary thing; she stood up and spoke out. In the end, as is my experience in all the crimes I have investigated or been a part of; evil is always trumped by good. The trouble is, a lot of damage is done along the way, before the scales tip.

Wake and Johnson were traced, implicated and never eliminated from this murder. The *Major Incident Room Standardised Administration Procedures Manual* which sets out this category of action is a technical book for detectives, but starts with a quote from Peter Abelard, a twelfth century French philosopher: 'The key to wisdom is by constant and frequent questioning, for by doubting we are led to questioning and by questioning we arrive at the truth.'

CHAPTER 18

Polo Pearson: The Dealer with the Hole in the Middle

During the summer of 1996 and during the height of the Russell Causley investigation, I appeared before a board of senior officers to be considered for promotion to the rank of superintendent. Many of my colleagues spent a considerable amount of time in researching various material and preparing in detail for such an event. Well, maybe they needed to. I was one of the most experienced DCIs in the force, I was in charge of all crime in the busiest division in Dorset and had a number of spectacularly good investigations under my belt; it was going to be a walkover. But it wasn't and my over inflated bubble of self-importance was not just pricked – it was lanced. I was graded 'C' meaning 'unfit for promotion'. I was absolutely staggered. How could that be so, especially as some of those judged 'fit for immediate promotion' had nowhere near my track record or experience. 'Experience', I was told, is not as important as what you are capable of doing in the future. I may have been a good DCI, but could I do the long-term strategic stuff demanded of superintendents? Apparently not.

Having picked myself up off the floor and determined to just 'bugger on', I gave it another crack the following year. This time I thought that I'd better play the game. I read all the right Home Office publications, and everything ever written by Her Majesty's Inspectorate of Constabulary. I spent a lot more time speaking with the more academic members of the Dorset Police intelligentsia. Tony Rogers, now a detective chief superintendent, called at my office and pointed me in the right direction and John Homer, also a chief superintendent, did the same. John was a great user of the latest buzz words. 'Take a helicopter view, Notty, come out of the nine dots,' he would say. I must have got something right in the end because I bumbled my way through the interview board and got an 'A' grade marking me as suitable for immediate promotion. How you can go from the one to the other in the space of twelve months, I don't know, but I wasn't going to make an issue of it. In early 1997, I got the dream job of being promoted to detective superintendent. I had responsibility for CID operations including the investigation of murder; responsibility for the management and use of informants and overall command of the criminal intelligence unit.

I shared being on call with another senior detective, John Campbell. In October 1997 I was at home with my wife when I received a call just after 9 pm. It was from Lynn Hart, the fighting sergeant from Christchurch, now a uniformed inspector at Bournemouth. She told me that there had been a shooting at a bedsit in Christchurch Road, Boscombe, and a man had been taken to hospital. I arrived at the apartment block about fifteen minutes later where I met Lynn who had done a good job of preserving the scene to protect forensic evidence and starting local enquiries to find witnesses. The scene of the crime was in an upper stairwell and landing within an Edwardian house typical of many of the properties in Boscombe once very fashionable but now quite run down. The facts as I was told were that the victim, a man in his twenties called Michael Pearson, had been at home with his girlfriend and, as I was later to find out, high as a kite on heroin. He answered a knock at the door and before anything was said he was shot in the stomach at very close range with a shotgun. In fact, the muzzle of the shotgun was so close to his stomach that the wadding from the gun was found imbedded in his stomach, with all the shot. Amazingly he was still alive but had only a fifty-fifty chance of surviving.

The house was sealed and guarded and a major investigation team assembled. At this time there were no standing major investigation teams ready to be deployed as Dorset didn't have the manpower or level of major crime to justify it. Cases like this were put together on the hoof. It may sound chaotic, but uniform and CID officers were all trained in the different disciplines required such as house to house enquiry teams, statement takers and investigators right through to family liaison officers and the operators and managers for the HOLMES computer system. Dorset Police officers were (and I am sure still are) able to be dropped into a murder, terrorist incident, plane crash, riot or other disaster and deal with it like it was their everyday job.

It is worth knowing how this group of specialists are coordinated. The computer system which records, analyses data and identifies matches within the system, is led by an office manager who in my experience was usually an experienced uniformed inspector. All statements, messages and documents which come into the incident room are read and actions raised by one or two detective sergeants. They read photocopies of all documents and underline them and mark on them the action to be taken such as 'take statement from Bloggs who was with the victim at the time of the attack'. Each action is given a unique number and entered into the computer system and cross referenced. The person who allocates this work and runs the enquiry team is usually an experienced detective inspector and called the action allocator. About ten uniformed officers are usually called in to carry out the house to house enquiries and a sergeant is in charge of them. On top of this are the crime scene team, intelligence officers (especially in a case like this) and other specialists. The victim's family are assigned a specially trained family liaison officer who is usually a detective constable who assists the family through the trauma of their loss. They are able to explain legal necessities such as the need for rigorous autopsies and obtain from the family the character and habits of the deceased. Any statements which need to be obtained from the family are accordingly taken by this officer, who is able to build a good rapport and provides a sensitive face from the criminal justice aspect. The investigation is led by a detective superintendent or detective chief inspector who is called the senior investigating officer (SIO). This role should be occupied by an experienced detective who should have been involved in numerous suspicious death or homicide investigations before being considered to take command at this level. They will also have attended a number of specialist high quality training courses and will have been accredited to lead investigations of this nature. It is the SIO's responsibility to instruct the issuing of orders to arrest suspects which will be taken after careful deliberation. When such arrests are to be made the SIO must note his or her reasons in the SIO's policy book. This is a record maintained by the SIO of all major decisions made during an enquiry together with the rationale for such decision with supporting reasons. This can be useful later when the investigation is reviewed for any number of reasons. This whole process is managed in accordance with the *Major Incident Room Standardised Administration Procedures Manual* as has already been mentioned.

County forces in general kept to this formula, but the Metropolitan Police did not always. Their manpower and commitment to major crimes had been cut back in the 1990s. When Stephen Lawrence was murdered in 1993, instead of deploying one or two detective sergeants as statement readers, an inspector as office manager and a detective inspector as action allocator, they allocated one detective sergeant to do all those jobs. No one police officer can possibly fulfil those roles efficiently in what should have been classified immediately as a category A murder. It is no wonder the investigation team missed vital clues in the first 'golden hours' of the crime. The fault, in my view, lay with the top leadership of the Met for failing to resource all murder enquiries properly, not just that one. There were also major tactical failures in dealing swiftly and decisively with multiple source information, which identified the killers of Stephen Lawrence within the first thirty-six hours.

In order to find the space needed for an incident room of twenty or so people I commandeered some offices in Bournemouth, belonging to an administrative department and we were soon whirring away with information coming in thick and fast. It was soon established that the victim was a low-level bedsit heroin dealer. These people are usually addicts themselves and have a small clientele of between ten to fifteen customers. They are all in the same social network group. They live hand to mouth stealing to get enough money for a hit (cost in the 1990s was about £90), zonk out, then steal to get the money for the next hit the following day. It is a dreadful life, and the cause of about seventy percent of all acquisitive crime at that time. The victim was in the operating theatre for hours whilst the surgeons worked with great skill and saved his life. I was told that it was believed he would have lost more blood and have been subject to the greater effects of shock had he not been high on heroin.

The first place to start was the scene of the crime. A small ball of heroin was found in the bloodstained clothing of the victim. A number of fingerprints were found in and around the scene but took time to identify; some of our well-known criminal friends lived in other bedsits within the block. It appeared no one saw anything whatsoever despite the loud report of a shotgun. So the victim was unconscious, his girlfriend and all the residents of the house saw nothing and there was no CCTV in the area at that time. We found one passing witness who saw two men exit the house after the shot, but he could not recognise them again or provide any description other than that they were men. This was clearly a drug or gang-related crime, so a good place to start was to check out all his associates. The drug community around the Crescent area of Boscombe was turned upside down.

The next day, as we were proceeding apace, we got a terrific break. Two uniformed officers from Hampshire had received a call to attend the Sandyballs Holiday Park near Fordingbridge in the New Forest. They had been called by the staff, who were suspicious about two men who had arrived the night before. The officers spoke to the two men and their policemen's sixth sense told them something wasn't right. They therefore searched their tent and found hidden under a blanket a twelve bore shotgun and cartridges. The officers checked the men's identity over the radio and it was revealed that they had criminal records which would disqualify them from possessing a gun. They were arrested and taken into Ringwood police station. The officers had heard on their briefing at 6am, just before they commenced their patrol, that there had been a shooting in Bournemouth and two men were believed to have been involved. The Hampshire officers phoned our incident room and asked if we were interested in the men they had arrested. A quick check with our criminal intelligence cell revealed that the two men, Kenneth Ian Gray and Francis John Halilowski, were known associates of the victim, and they were involved in the Boscombe drug scene. We were very interested indeed.

The intelligence cell uncovered that Gray and Halilowski had been renting a flat in Churchill Gardens, Boscombe, a distance of about a quarter of a mile from the scene of the crime in Christchurch Road. We also knew the car they had been using, the colour of which was a faded shade of red. A search of the flat they had been living in was quickly made and two shotgun cartridges were recovered, being of the same batch which had been found in their possession. Unfortunately, no finger prints were found on the cartridges.

Our excitement started to stall over the next day. Both men refused to answer questions, there was no forensic evidence at the scene, and we had no witnesses who could identify them. The victim was still too ill and was unable to identify his assailants as their faces were covered. The only thing we did have was a match with the shotgun ammunition. The shot and wadding dug out of Mr Pearson's abdomen was exactly the same shot and wadding as to be found in the shot gun cartridges found in the possession of Gray and Halilowski. Unfortunately, due to the smooth bore of a shotgun and the fact that the shot comprises small balls fired through a larger barrel, no marks sufficient for court purposes are made on the projectiles. So that was it; we seemed to be going nowhere and our custody time limits (twenty-four hours for most offences and thirty-six hours for a serious offence like this) were running out. I was able to charge one of the men with illegal possession of the shotgun and keep him in custody, but the second man I had to let go.

I had one last chance. I had attended a course at the senior police training college at Bramshill in Hampshire called the 'Serious and Series Crime Course,' probably the best course ever provided by the police. This was a two-week study of all recent murders and major crimes and presented by senior investigating officers. The greatest value of the course was where those senior detectives confided the areas in which they had got it wrong, or made mistakes. I learned a lot and one thing of particular relevance; in a close quarter shooting, blood can end up in a specific place on the gun. In the case of Jeremy Bamber, who murdered five members of his own family in 1985, blood from the victims was found on a shotgun he had access to in a specific place on the weapon. Following this hunch, I spoke to the Crime Scene Manager, Terry Marsden and told him of my thoughts. Terry was for many years the senior forensic crime scene examiner in Dorset and very accomplished. He was a quiet, suave, well-dressed, gentlemanly sort of man with a wry sense of humour. He advised me that my theory was a possibility, and he would be able get the gun to the laboratory in Chepstow within hours. He would request the forensic scientist with responsibility for ballistics to work through the night, if necessary, to complete the examination in the short time frame I needed. As usual there was a catch, it would cost me £2000 which was a massive chunk out of the budget I had been allocated. 'Okay, Terry, let's do it.' It was the only thing we had, and we all held our breath.

That same evening at around 9 pm I went with a few of the team to Churchill Gardens to make a frantic attempt to find anyone who was in that vicinity a few evenings earlier, in the hope they saw our suspects leaving the flat. Fortuna was once again at my side because by sheer luck I approached a girl of about eighteen years standing literally on a street corner, and as I discovered, selling herself for a shot of heroin. I told her she had nothing to fear and that we were the police. I asked her if she had been here two days earlier at the same time. Straight away she said that she had, and when questioned further told me that she had seen two men come out from a house up the road and get into a faded red colour car. She thought she would be able to recognise them again. This was a poor kid, hooked on heroin, doing the most demeaning things to get her next fix, but she was prepared to stand up and be counted; more so than some other esteemed members of the community I would say, a number of whom would consider her trash.

The next day was the big wait. We had arrested the second man again on the strength of our young witness. The young damaged heroin addict and prostitute attended an identification parade and picked out the two thugs in a line up. She had nothing to gain herself, nor has she ever received any real credit for helping identify two would-be killers. But it still wasn't enough, all we could prove was that they had left their flat five minutes before the shooting. Then the call came in from the laboratory. I took it. The whole team looked on; they knew it was all or nothing: It was everything, blood was discovered on a very specific part of the shotgun found in our suspects possession at Sandyballs camp site. A complete DNA match was made with the victim; our suspects were fried. We had got them. An almighty cheer went up and it was that time again for me to delve deep into my pockets and pay for the first round of drinks in the police club for the whole team. Kenneth Ian Gray and Francis John Halilowski were subsequently convicted at the Crown Court of the shooting and sentenced to substantial terms of imprisonment

I visited Mr Pearson in hospital as he recovered. He was quite a nice bloke actually, as was his girlfriend. They were just two kids sucked into the dark world of drugs. He called heroin his demon. It woke up with him every day, nagged him to be fed and haunted him continually. He badly wanted to give it up. I lost touch with him and his girlfriend after the case; I hope he won his battle. The poem below – 'The White Horse' – was written by Paul, a Bournemouth addict who lost his battle with the demon.

At the conclusion of the case I was presented with a plaque from my jocular team, it was a comic book male character on a wooden board. The figure's stomach was a polo mint and it was entitled 'Senior Investigating Officer – Polo Pearson the Dealer with The Hole in The Middle'.

> Come ride the white horse, the horse dealer cried
> You'll have a good trip, he cruelly lied.
> The first rides for free, those words did the trick
> I rode off on his back, but after felt sick.

The next time I saw him, I asked after his horse
I wanted to ride, so he said but of course.
He charged me a score, which seemed pretty mean
But I rode off to heaven, where I'd never been.

When the journey was over, the horse brought me back
To a new hell on earth, where I'd need more smack.
I said to the horse dealer, I begged him for more
After that he came to my door.

The horse ran from heaven and to hell with my soul
I was no longer master, the horse had control.
The dealer looked different, horns hoofs and tail
Upon my return, a guaranteed sale.

Fixed up once more, to the heavens I rode
I tried chasing dragon, it cost me much gold.
White horses' cost plenty, my money had gone
So, I stole for my habit, though I knew it were wrong.

In prison, white horses aren't allowed in
I cried in pain and my body grew thin.
So, this is my story, of my horse-riding days
Left with nothing but memories and a confusing haze.

So, if you ride white horses, please ride them well
Because the white horses, will take you to hell.

CHAPTER 19

Obsession

April 1998 was the month in which Sinn Fein signed the 'Good Friday Agreement', bringing thirty years of bloodshed in Northern Ireland and mainland Britain to a stuttering end. The IRA 'troubles' had occupied much of my police service from attending bomb explosions in central London in the early seventies through to being the CID Commander at Labour and Conservative conferences in Bournemouth. The IRA only visited us once in Dorset to do damage. This was in 1985, when they set a bomb off on the pier and caused fire damage to three shops with incendiary devices. Apart from that, we trained and practised, but were mercifully spared the full horror the IRA could bring. In October 1998 they made their last big attack at Omagh in Northern Ireland killing twenty-nine people who had been out shopping and enjoying themselves. The victims included Spanish students, women and children. The IRA failed to realise that making war on innocent civilians achieved nothing.

On Wednesday 2 April I was working in my office at Police Headquarters, Winfrith. The buildings were originally part of the Atomic Energy (experimental) Establishment and had been purchased by the Dorset Police. The HQ was surrounded by fields and always seemed remote from the buzz of the busy police stations I had worked in. The police out in the towns and boroughs frequently referred to HQ as 'Turnip Towers' or on occasions 'Jurassic Park'. I got a call from DI Martin Holloway, my old best man who was stationed in Bournemouth. The body of a young woman had been found in a flat next to her own apartment above a parade of shops in Kinson, a large sprawling council estate on the northern edge of the town. She had appeared to have died from massive head injuries. Forensic officers were on the way and another detective inspector was pulling together staff for the enquiry. I jumped into my car and drove to the scene, but I wasn't really ready for what I was about to see. I entered the apartment with Martin and saw, in the lounge, lying on her back, the body of Michele Lock. Her head had been literally smashed in on one side with the skull crushed to the lower jaw. She was naked from the waist down. The whole living room was like a slaughter house, with blood splashed on virtually every wall and ceiling, because Michele had been struck multiple times with a very heavy blunt object. I was told that she was a single woman aged twenty-eight. She was very well known and liked in the locality and had a penchant for ale of all kinds and was a regular at 'Gulliver's' one of the principal pubs for Kinson folk. She also had a taste for herbal tobacco. Her parents were well established locals and a family liaison officer (FLO) had been assigned to them. I was told it was to be WDC Sandy Robertson, a very experienced detective who had also been the FLO in the Du Rose case. I was immediately concerned. The role of FLO, while always one where the officer maintains a business-like police head, is also extremely draining. The job entails virtually living with the family, or at least staying permanently connected. The impact of such sudden and unwarranted death on a family is devastating and the FLO will become infected by the grief; they are human, after all. I felt that Sandy had had enough of this with recent cases as she was a popular choice for the role. However, and fortunately, I was aware that we had just trained a fresh batch of officers and I suggested to my colleague in a tactful way that perhaps we needed to skill up somebody else, so two fresh detectives were assigned the case and Sandy was spared – not that she wouldn't have made a first-class job of dealing with the family.

Next, I went to Bournemouth Central police station and started making sure we had sufficient staff. Once again, I had to prise officers out of the hands of Divisional commanders, with the usual suspects being more awkward than others. Martin Holloway very quickly got the murder squad busy and arranged for a search team to comb the dustbins and drains in the surrounding locality. Our initial prime suspect was the on-off boyfriend of Michele who was seen to leave her apartment that morning as the police arrived next door at the murder scene. He was a well-known local tough, handy with his fists and with a susceptibility for heavy drinking. She had also had another boyfriend who had recently been trying to see her and he was also known for violence. This lady had not had an easy life. A team was assigned to investigate the possibility that her boyfriend had killed her in a fit of rage following a domestic row. Domestic violence frequently accelerates into murder especially where violence becomes commonplace. I was told as a young bobby that every 'domestic' is a potential murder and always treated them as such. Unfortunately, the police forget this golden rule occasionally with terrible consequences. One of the first things I asked to be checked was 'do we have a record of domestic violence against Michele'? Fortunately, we did not, and therefore had not neglected her. The Home Office pathologist who visited the scene estimated the time of Michele's death at between 9pm on 1 April and 7am 2 April.

Despite any direct evidence, the circumstances were such that I instructed a trace implicate or eliminate (TIE) action be created on Michelle's boyfriend. We needed to rule him in, or rule him out, one way or another. He was soon located, arrested and subjected to a thorough medical and forensic examination. He had seen Michele the day before, that is Tuesday 1 April and was in Gulliver's public house until about ten to eight that evening. One witness who had been in the pub described an argument between the two. Significantly, CCTV footage recovered from the pub showed them kissing just before Michele left. The boyfriend stayed on at the pub but tried to see Michele later the same evening. He went to her apartment, but she was not there. He used her land line phone at about 1150 pm that evening to try to locate her at various friends' houses but couldn't find her. When he was arrested, he was wearing the same clothes he had been seen wearing in the pub the day before. The car which he had used the previous evening was checked by scenes of crimes officers and no blood stains whatsoever were found. His alibi for that whole evening was checked in detail and found to be true, and furthermore despite his hard-man reputation, he was devastated by the death of Michele.

While this was in progress the enquiry team had to unravel why Michele's body was found in the apartment where she was and not at home, and where was the occupier of that premises, Simon Coombe? Murder enquiries do not focus on one suspect at a time. Where suspects appear in an investigation separate lines of enquiry are established and a team deployed to that suspect. The enquiry as a whole trundles on, hoovering up all the facts and data available and creating further lines as it goes. A number of suspects can be in the frame and being worked on simultaneously, an SIO will never put all his/her eggs in one basket.

The police control room had received information that same day from a local psychiatric hospital that a past patient, Simon Coombe, had called that morning to see his former psychiatrist. He told him that he found Michele's body the evening before in his flat and explained to the doctor that he had spent some time with her in his flat drinking and enjoying sex with her. He went out for some fresh air and a walk and when he returned, he found her dead, having been subject to a violent attack. He said that he panicked and left his flat and walked around Bournemouth before deciding to visit his psychiatrist the next morning. He told the psychiatrist that he was worried the police would try to pin the killing on him. The Control Room immediately despatched officers to speak to Mr Coombe, but by the time they got to the hospital he had gone. Furious efforts to trace him were then put in hand.

The hunt to find Simon Coombe ended much quicker than expected. He had made his way to his solicitor's office opposite Bournemouth police station in Lansdowne Road and was talking to him when officers were searching throughout Bournemouth. Despite issues around solicitor/client confidentiality, the solicitor decided that due to the disclosures being made, the police should be informed. The solicitor's secretary contacted the police and within minutes, Mr Coombe was in custody for murder. We had two completely different suspects in custody for a murder involving different scenarios and for which only one could have been responsible, but both were in or near the scene during the relevant times.

Simon Coombe, an insignificant looking youth in his twenties, was subjected to the standard forensic examination before he was interviewed. This was carried out by the Police Surgeon and a Scenes of Crimes (CSI) officer. His clothes bore no blood stains but there was a pattern of blood staining on his socks. It was noticed he had two scratch marks to his left cheek and a recent bruise to the right side of his neck. He was then interviewed at length by two experienced detectives. While the SIO is an experienced CID officer if he/she became involved in interviewing suspects they would lose control of the rest of the enquiry. Furthermore, it should be remembered that interviewing suspects is a great skill and detective constables and detective sergeant are engaged on this on an almost daily basis. They therefore maintain their edge which is vital. In murder cases, it is usual for a detective inspector to 'manage' the interview after consultation with the SIO thus maintaining a structured approach to the investigation in which an overall strategy and tactics are worked out in advance.

Coombe explained to the officers that he had met Michele Lock on the evening of Tuesday 1 April and had invited her into his apartment for a drink. He said that she was more than willing, and they very quickly became entangled in passionate love making. He claimed that she had accidentally scratched his face and bruised his neck in her ardour for him and he had full sex with her. He said that it was she who dragged him into the lounge where after a while she fell asleep, and he went out for some fresh air and a walk. He continued that it was after he returned that he found her dead, and he panicked and left the apartment. He explained the blood staining on his socks as being as a result of walking across the floor without his training shoes on after his return from his walk. He was unable to answer why he should have taken his shoes off, and later thought he was wearing his shoes. He explained the cut to his ear as being the result of Michele ripping his earring off in her passion. Needless to say, the interviewers were unconvinced by these answers.

Simultaneously to the questioning of both Coombe and Michele's boyfriend, the search teams deployed by Martin Holloway were having success. In a paladin refuse bin at the back of the parade of shops near the scene of the crime, officers had recovered a blood-stained pipe cutter. This was a metal device about two feet long with one end being particularly heavy and weighing over two kilos (2.4lb). In another refuse bin officers found a pair of jeans and top garment also heavily bloodstained.

Officers carrying out house to house enquiries around the scene were able to build up a picture of the movements of both Michele and Coombe. She had been drinking with her boyfriend in Gulliver's pub that evening as previously mentioned. The pub was not far from her apartment and she was tracked from the pub which she left at about 8 pm towards her home. She was seen collapsed (drunk) at the foot of the stairs leading to her apartment a little later by a neighbour who saw a man talking to Michele which was believed to be Coombe. Coombe was seen to go into an off-licence near his apartment at around 8 pm and buy a four pack of lager. Examination of CCTV footage showed Coombe wearing clothing identical to that found in the refuse bin.

The evidence was now beginning to stack up. We had an initial account from Coombe which was beginning to look like a fantasy, the boyfriend was beginning to be alibied out, we had bloodstained clothing which appeared to belong to Coombe, and we had the murder weapon. The balance had tilted in our favour. Next enter the forensic scientist. Our CSI chief, Terry Marsden, brought down an expert in blood splattering from the Forensic Science Service Laboratory. I had lost some confidence in this science following the lack of a decisive result in the murder of Paul Bradshaw. However, the scientist was able to determine with confidence by the shape of blood spattering found that the jeans and top, and importantly the socks, were worn by someone standing by the victim at the moment the impact blows were being made to the victim. Blood spray and splashes exhibit certain characteristics which scientifically prove where a person was standing as blows are inflicted. Drops of blood fly through the air from their source in the shape of a tiny ball. As the droplet hits a surface the droplet acts like a wave and the greater part of the droplet flops over, spreading the larger area of blood away from the direction of travel. The 'sharp point' of the tear drop points to the direction from where the impact occurred. Fine spray is also given off where a person is beaten excessively, as in this case. The spray travels only a short distance so any person with this pattern of spray on them must have been very close to the victim when the injuries were inflicted. The scientist took the trouble of giving a mini lecture on this subject in the incident room to the education of all of us.

Coombe was again interviewed as a result of the new evidence and began to adapt his defence to the evidence as it was presented. He finally adopted a no comment approach as the evidence began to overwhelm him. Differences in his story also began to appear in what he had told the psychiatrist to whom he had first fled. He told him that he had spent the day with Michele before a romantic evening turned into a sexual fest. He told the police that he called on Michele after 8 pm after she had returned from the pub and he from the off-licence. Witnesses told the police that since Michele had suffered a tragic miscarriage, she didn't rate sex; she was definitely not a promiscuous woman at all. In fact, the earring which she obviously tore off Coombe's ear was found in the hall way just inside his front door. The picture was emerging of a stalker who had become obsessed about Michele, luring her into his flat with cans of lager and attempting to rape her. She obviously fought like a tigress, but he smashed her head in with the pipe cutter, which police were later to prove had been left in the apartment by a previous tenant. Semen stains around her vagina and thighs were evidence of the sexual activity, but unfortunately and despite our very strong views, the Crown Prosecution Service felt there was insufficient evidence to charge rape. We also found a friend of Michele's who told us that she viewed Coombe as 'that creepy bastard next door'.

Digging into the background of Coombe we uncovered a man with a manipulative personality who had used violence on women before. He broke one young woman's wrist and dominated others. He also obsessed about sex claiming to have made love to other young women who denied anything had ever happened. He also fantasised and boasted to some friends that he had killed police officers in America and was a clear fan of Sharon Stone and some of his antics mirrored scenes from the film *Basic Instinct*. The total sum of separate sightings of the pair by witnesses, CCTV pictures, recovered bloodstained clothing, and the forensic evidence proved to be so overwhelming that when he appeared at Bournemouth Crown Court in March 1999, he pleaded guilty to murder and was jailed for life. Coombe had had a troubled psychiatric life in his past having been a patient at a psychiatric hospital in Poole. After his release he failed to keep appointments with doctors and went on to kill in the most horrific manner. Coombe was not insane when he committed these offences but deemed by the court to know the difference between right and wrong. Once again, I found myself asking when does mental illness become nothing other than an evil personality? Mental illness affects many people, but it is an illness; evil is something different and illness can be something to hide behind. Look at the cases of Fred and Rose West who possessed undiluted evil. Martin Holloway went to see Coombe whilst he was serving his prison sentence to ask him for an explanation for his barbaric behaviour. Martin found him still in denial and without remorse.

CHAPTER 20

Murder and Problems with Timing

Murder when viewed from the aspect of the trial can appear fairly straight forward. The facts are laid out by barristers in a coherent manner and form a logical sequence of events from the commission of the crime, the presentation of witnesses in a chronological sequence, through to the arrest interview and charge of the accused. However, as has already been shown in this book that is not how the matter unfolds to the detective. There are many occasions when a body has been found that the cause of death can-not be readily ascertained. This can only be satisfactorily achieved by an autopsy and other tangible enquiry concerning the known facts and medical history. It is absolutely crucial that assumptions are not made; this is a golden rule of crime investigation. The next case illustrates just how important this rule is.

On Wednesday 9 September 1998 I was at home with my wife in Christchurch. We were watching the highlights of the World Cup and witnessed the depressing sight of England losing to Argentina and being knocked out of the competition on penalties (again). The phone went, and my wife expelled a sigh.

It was the control room. 'Hello, sir, can you attend 2, King Street, Bridport? A man has been found dead in his house. He has an injury to his head. Scenes of Crimes are on their way.'

Bridport is a picturesque market town at the western edge of Dorset surrounded by rolling lush green hills, close to the magnificent coastal town of Lyme Regis, and has a fairly static, close community. I drove the fifty miles to Bridport arriving over an hour later. The scene of the crime was a one-bedroom house in the centre of the town; the building was about eighty to a hundred years old, which is comparatively modern for the area.

Upon arrival I met the Scenes of Crimes team who had already started making some preliminary investigations. These included laying aluminium stepping plates from the front door to the corpse, which was situated about eight feet inside the door, and lying on the floor of the kitchen. The deceased was Ken Webber, a well-built local man in his fifties, and the sole occupant of the house. His body had been discovered earlier that evening by his son, who, when receiving no answer to the door bell, looked through the letter box and saw his father lying on the floor. He called the police and ambulance straight away. The door was locked with a Yale type lock and there was no sign of a forced entry. The downstairs lights were on, and the house was in good order with little sign of disturbance. The ambulance service attended, but they found that Mr Webber had been dead for some time. He was in a slightly rigid state believed to be rigor mortis receding. I was informed at the scene by a highly qualified scientific officer that rigor mortis sets in after four hours and goes out after twenty-four to thirty-six hours. It is not uncommon for the forensic examiners to request the attendance to the scene of a forensic scientist with certain specialisms, in this case pathology. It being Wednesday, just after nine in the evening, death could be estimated as having occurred some-time the previous day, from the morning onwards at a very rough guess. So, our investigation could be based on the assumption that he had died some-time on the Tuesday. As good detectives know, you can't assume anything, but in this case, I assumed the science was correct.

Being the Senior Investigating Officer, I was one of the few people who could enter the scene. The only break in the tidy order of the house was a spice rack which had fallen from the kitchen work surface onto the floor. Mr Webber himself was lying face down and had cuts and bruises to his face and lips, but little other evidence of excessive violence. The strangest injury was a two centimetre cut to his head which bore no sign of blood flow or bruising. There was also a tuft of hair on his head which appeared to have been cut with a very sharp instrument. Very close to his head was a whisky tumbler, the rim of which was broken, jagged and sharp, but had no blood stains on it. On the floor of the living room close to the body was the screw cap of a Glenfiddich bottle. The bottle itself was on a windowsill upstairs outside a bedroom. Mr Webber was wearing a jacket which had partly come off, one arm in and one arm out and his shirt had been pulled outside his trousers which were partly pulled down. There was a graze on his stomach, but no other signs of injury. It appeared he could have been dragged to the position in which the body had been found, but the injuries which I saw were far too slight to have caused his death. The wound on his head was a puzzle; it looked odd. Another strange thing was to see an empty Budweiser bottle just outside the front door on a low wall. Was it left there by Mr Webber or someone who had been helping him? The scenes of crimes officers would spend over a week, working eight hours a day to complete their examination of the scene. Every door, wall and surface would be examined for fingerprints and other body residue. Sheets, bedding and carpets would be subject to minute examination. Not one tiny clue must escape their meticulous, and sometimes mind-numbing examination.

Mr Webber was a divorced man in his late fifties, quite heavily built, and considered locally to be a heavy drinker. My first thought was that he had suffered a heart attack, knocked the spice rack over and fallen on the glass cutting his head. My second option was that he had collapsed outside his house perhaps intoxicated and was dragged home by a well-meaning drinking partner and had died on the floor, perhaps by choking on his own vomit. But that cut on his head didn't seem right. My instinct was to play it safe, and all those injuries to the face could be more than just superficial bruising caused when being dragged home. I thought it best to get our resident Home Office Pathologist, Doctor Anscombe, in on this one and have a full forensic autopsy. It was going to cost my CID budget over a thousand pounds, but I knew my boss Desi Donohoe would support me, although very likely to give me a dressing down lightly garnished with some micky taking in private if I was wrong.

The house was sealed until after the result of the autopsy, and uniformed officers maintained a guard on the scene. The officers maintained a log of all people entering and leaving the scene to which access is strictly limited. At the same time a major investigation team was earmarked and put on standby. The next day, Thursday, Doctor Anscombe carried out the autopsy and very quickly discovered that Mr Webber had died from massive internal injuries. He felt that these injuries could have been caused by a road accident, possibly a lorry backing into him; a fall from at least ten feet or more onto a wall or scaffolding pole, or indeed by a severe kicking, even though there were no shoe or boot imprints on the body. If he had been assaulted, Doctor Anscombe stressed that the injuries would have been sustained by more than punches, more likely multiple violent kicks and possibly being jumped up and down on. He believed the cut I described as 'strange' on his head to have been caused at least thirty minutes after death. I didn't really know what we had and trying to tell my chief constable why I was setting up a major enquiry was not easy, because I didn't know what on earth we were investigating. I secretly thought this was a road accident and that he had been dragged home by his friends. I had dealt with a similar case to this some years earlier, where an alcoholic had fallen over after a heavy drinking session, only to be dragged home by well-meaning friends, and further serious injuries were unwittingly caused which resulted in total paralysis.

That afternoon (Thursday) a full enquiry team to investigate a 'cold start' murder had been collected together in the local CID office at Bridport police station. This included a full HOLMES computer system as described earlier, together with trained operators. I had my own close team comprising the local Detective Inspector, Simon Hester, and Detective Chief Inspector Dave King, the senior CID officer in west Dorset.

The first thing I did was to prepare a press release. We needed witnesses badly, and if this was a tragic accident, an appeal had to be made for any innocent party involved in taking Mr Webber home to come forward. I prepared a press release which I read over to my top team. I guess I emphasised the road accident and fall primarily and mentioned the possibility of an assault as an afterthought. My deputy was Dave King, whom I had first worked with in Weymouth when we were both detective constables. Dave was a rotund chap, highly energetic and quick witted, who spoke in a loud, confident manner. He had a copy of my intended press release which he read again and said to me, 'You haven't made enough on the assault side of this, Governor; sounds too much like an RTA' (Road Traffic Accident, now called a Road Traffic Collision).

I read the draft press release again, 'Police are investigating the unexplained death of Mr Ken Webber who is believed to have died between twelve noon on Tuesday 8th to the evening of Wednesday 9th September 1998.'

I gave details of where he was found and the cause of death, the massive trauma injuries to the abdomen. I crossed out the too few words I had written about an assault and rewrote it to give much more emphasis to the possibility that he had been beaten and kicked to death. Dave was right; I had been too eager to think this was an accident.

Next, I had to brief the officers assembling in the general CID office at Bridport police station which had been commandeered for the duration of the investigation. This took place early in the afternoon of Thursday 10 September. Briefings are an important part of a major crime enquiry and in the early stages held once in the morning and then around 6 pm in the evening when officers are in for refreshments. The first few days are manic; the flow of paper and information can become dizzying as the enquiry twists and turns with huge amounts of data being acquired. The feedback from the officers employed on the outside enquiries and HOLMES operators is vital to the SIO, as he/she tries to knit together the facts. I have more than once heard a uniformed or detective constable make a suggestion to the SIO (often 20 years or more senior in experience) during a briefing which has proved to be the identity of the killer or a line of enquiry which leads to them. No SIO ever ignores the suggestions and comments from the floor – usually very experienced officers in their own right – but the trick is spotting the gem in the routine and continuing to provide a safe environment for sound ideas to be suggested. I outlined to the enquiry team the facts as we knew them so far.

Two local Bridport CID officers, Tim Bugler and Ian Roach, then added their local knowledge into the mix. Following the discovery of the body of Mr Webber on Wednesday evening they visited several town centre pubs. Not far from the house of Mr Webber was the Lord Nelson Public House in East Street. Mr Webber was well known there as a regular customer and heavy drinker. During the evening of Monday 7 September, he was seen in the bar talking to a young man wearing a baseball cap which was worn back to front. The local Bridport folk were a bit wary of a person dressed like that and took particular note. Mr Webber was seen to leave the pub at about 10.30 pm by the landlady in the company of the youth wearing the baseball cap. A little later the youth was seen to return, and he bought a bottle of Budweiser with a £50 note and left shortly thereafter. That was the last sighting of Mr Webber alive. Whilst I was still working on Tuesday 8 September as his time of death, this sighting was clearly significant especially as the youth had bought a bottle of Budweiser. The landlady was later to recall that she could see Mr Webber's house from her pub and noticed his lights were still on at 3.00 am and she even noticed a bottle of whisky in an upstairs windowsill. The tracing of this youth had become a high priority.

That afternoon, (Thursday 10 September) officers managed to track down this youth, Richard Hawkes, a shop fitter who was working with a group of men from the home counties on a shop in the high street. He was questioned about his movements on the Monday evening and was happy to tell the police that he had been in the Lord Nelson on the Monday night where he had met an old man. He told them he had been invited back to his house where he had drunk a glass of whisky with him, but he said that he didn't stay long. His work mates were also questioned that Thursday evening, but added little more than what Mr Hawkes had said.

As Thursday drew on, an anonymous note was delivered to the incident room, in which it was claimed that Mr Webber was a homosexual who frequented public toilets looking for sexual partners. The family liaison officer was tasked to follow this up with his family and discreetly ask, if they knew if he was a homosexual who looked for sexual contacts in this way; they did not, and this came as a complete surprise. Furthermore, and just to complicate things, the incident room received reports of sightings of Mr Webber alive and well in various locations in Bridport on the Tuesday and Wednesday of that week. Add to this a desire for answers from senior officers at headquarters and questions from the press; I was beginning to wish I had remained in the civil service as a tax gatherer.

Friday was decision day. The shop fitters would finish work at about 3.00 pm and return to their homes in and around London. Any forensic evidence still available would be lost. If Hawkes had killed Mr Webber, he would be psychologically stronger thinking he had got away with it. We also discovered that whilst Mr Webber was an alcoholic with dark sexual secrets, he was a valued chef at a nearby holiday camp. We learned from his employers that he had been asked on the Monday if he would work on Tuesday. It would have been extra hours for him and he needed the money, so he agreed. We were told that he was a very reliable worker and if he promised to work a shift, he would not let his employers down and report in. He didn't turn up for work that Tuesday morning and had not made contact to say why he could not work, which was all highly unusual.

The time of death, which I had been led to believe was Tuesday morning at the earliest, was now looking questionable. Estimating the time of death is not a precise science and can have a number of variables including temperature. Confusion over times of death have led in the past to miscarriages of justice. In April 1972, Maxwell Confait was found dead in his flat which had also been set on fire. The time of his death was crucial because the three prime suspects had alibis before and after the time of death estimated by the pathologist, but not for the precise time he was believed to have been killed. The three suspects, who were all local youths, were charged and convicted in relation to his killing. After considerable efforts by the defence team, and indeed politicians, the case was referred back to the Court of Appeal. Mistakes by the pathologist concerning the time of death, (due in part to night storage heaters affecting temperatures) and other concerns regarding the investigation were cited among the reasons by the Court of Appeal when they returned a verdict quashing the convictions against the three youths.

Mindful of this case, which was ingrained in the minds of senior detectives, I decided to be a little flexible on the time of death until I could get more qualified scientific opinion. I therefore ruled Monday in as the possible day he died. It was then necessary for me to update the SIO's policy book accordingly. This is a log kept by the SIO which contains all significant decisions made during the course of a major enquiry. Key parameters such as the time of death, description of suspect, and decisions to arrest certain individuals must always be noted in the policy book, and, importantly, the rationale behind those actions.

As the detectives on the enquiry team visited and took statements from everybody connected with the victim, including friends and family, a possible scenario was building in my mind. A young man met the victim in a nearby pub. He went with the victim to his house on the Monday night and drank whisky. Did they both go upstairs to a bedroom with the whisky bottle for a sexual encounter? Could Hawkes have killed Mr Webber in a ferocious attack because he was disgusted with his advances, and may be his own inclinations? Fifteen minutes later he returned to the pub and bought a bottle of Budweiser and disappeared again; was that when the post mortem wound on the head was caused? After the first anonymous note had been received in the incident room a picture was established of Mr Webber being known as 'cottager'; a colloquial slang term for a man who seeks casual sex with other men in and around public toilets. I felt with some alarm that the timing of death had to be wrong. It had been cold over those few days; perhaps rigor mortis stayed in longer. The sightings of the victim on Tuesday and Wednesday had to be wrong, and time was running out.

There was only one course of action open. I created a TIE (Trace Implicate or Eliminate) action on Hawkes. I felt that I lacked all the ingredients to classify him as a suspect, his workmates had put him in the clear and there was a strong scientific argument against the time of death being Monday evening. However, the time of death could be wrong, and Hawkes had put himself with Mr Webber that evening. Was the cottager with the secret life tempted to make physical advances against a young fit man which thereby triggered a violent reaction? There was clearly a strong need to either implicate Hawkes by forensic evidence and that of witnesses or alternatively eliminate him by forensic evidence, or other provable means – CCTV for example. His work mates also needed to be spoken to again, this time at the police station.

Without delay that Friday morning, the 11 September, Hawkes and three shop fitters were 'invited' into Bridport police station to 'help us with our enquiries'. Each shop fitter was assigned two detectives who questioned them in detail. Whilst Hawkes stuck to his original story, cracks appeared elsewhere. The workmen had by now realised that this was a murder enquiry, and having no particular allegiance to Hawkes, decided that it was time to tell the truth. One man told the officers how on the Monday night Hawkes, with whom he was sharing a room, came into the hotel bedroom sometime after 10.00 pm and told him he had been touched up (indecently assaulted) by a man who deserved a beating. Telling him to be quiet, the workman went back to sleep, but noticed Hawkes have a shower before going to bed. That was something he did not usually do. He was again woken up later on when Hawkes again came into the room, (obviously having gone out again) and said that he had given the man a 'good kicking' and broken his arm. The following morning the group of workmen walked past Mr Webber's house on the way to the shop they were refurbishing in the high street. Hawkes pointed out Mr Webber's house to his workmates and told them that that was where the man lived who he had beaten up. He was limping at the time which he said was due to him kicking the man. The workmen later said that they thought the victim was probably just a bit sore around the ribs and didn't realise he had died.

As Hawkes's world fell in around him, he admitted what he had done; well, in part anyway. He told the interviewing officers detectives Bugler and Roach, (they had earned the right to be interviewing officers as they had developed this lead to start with) that he had beaten Mr Webber because of unwanted homosexual advances. He said that after arriving at the victim's house they drank whisky together in the lounge, but he failed to account why the whisky bottle was upstairs and the cap of the bottle and glasses were downstairs. He said that after he had punched and kicked the victim, he went back to his hotel room and had a shower; he didn't say why. He then went back to the victim's house and found him lifeless where he had left him on the tarmac outside the front door. He added this in his last interview, and it was clear that it was outside, near a small car park, where the major attack was launched. After returning he dragged the body back inside the house and dropped it on the floor near (or onto) the broken glass. Scientific evidence was obtained which stated that the glass could have caused the post mortem head injury. Equally a suggestion was offered from the pathologist that it could have been caused by a chisel-shaped object as a fracture to the skull was found under this cut, which indicated it was inflicted with some force. Was the injury caused by a brick hammer or other builder's tool to deliver a coup de grace? We will never know; the trouble with real murder cases is that loose ends often remain unanswered.

One whole bundle of loose ends which did need explaining was that twelve people had seen Ken Webber alive on the Tuesday and Wednesday after Hawkes had admitted killing him. I assigned this bugger's muddle of a complication to Detective Sergeant Morns. Steve Morns is a typical country detective, he had a strong Dorset accent, would say muff instead of mouth as in Weymuff or Bournemuff; he had an unassuming nature, a unique dress sense, and possessed a deep-thinking head. He wrote in near copperplate handwriting and had an enormous appetite for work unsurpassed by anyone. He put his meticulous mind to the task of examining this puzzle and came back to me a day or two later puffing on his pipe.

'You know what, Guv? I've had statements taken from all these witnesses some of whom knew him well, but guess what? Nobody actually talked to him, these were sightings only.'

Steve had a done his usual thorough job. He had read all the statements from the witnesses and had broken them down into three categories. The first group were people who had seen the victim in places he was known to be a day or two earlier, for example outside his house, or standing at a bus stop. The second group had sighted him in various places in Bridport High Street, and the third group saw him in and around a betting shop. When the first group were seen again, they confessed that because their sightings were a few days earlier they could have muddled up the exact day. On the sightings in the High Street, Steve had recovered CCTV footage which revealed a person in the places the witnesses had said they had seen the victim, but it was not Mr Webber; it was in fact someone who closely resembled him. And the third group who had made the sightings in and around the bookies had seen another man who also closely resembled Mr Webber. This man had placed a bet and was subsequently traced by Steve's team and he made a statement confirming his presence at the betting shop at the relevant times; he was very similar in age and appearance to our victim and this was another case of mistaken identity. So the last group of sightings were put to bed. The skill displayed by Steve is bread and butter detective work, which is to painstakingly read massive amounts of material and discern patterns and characteristics in the mist of words.

The trial commenced in late April 1999. Hawkes admitted that he was responsible for the death of Mr Webber but denied intentionally killing him. Hawkes told the court that he had met the victim in the Lord Nelson pub and gone back to his home with him. He alleged that Mr Webber had groped him, and he fought him off. In the struggle Mr Webber fell to the ground, and he admitted kicking him twice to the stomach. Hawkes told the court that he did this because he was in fear of being raped. This did not add up however, as the attack took place outside the front door adjacent to the public car park. The victim of course could not speak for himself. But the pathologist could and he was able to show that the injuries to Mr Webber were savage and included a broken nose, jaw, fractured arm and broken ribs with death resulting from massive internal bleeding. Mr Webber's body told its own story. Christopher Wilson-Smith QC, prosecuting, told Winchester Crown Court 'This was a savage, sustained attack on a much older man who had drunk a great deal.'

On Friday 7 May 1999 the jury having considered the defence by Hawkes that he had only kicked Mr Webber twice, decided to accept the arguments of Mr Wilson-Smith QC and returned a verdict of guilty to murder.

After Hawkes was sentenced to the mandatory term of life imprisonment, I spoke to a close relative of his who had come to collect some of his belongings. He was an older man who I suspect had a great deal of influence over the young Hawkes. Whilst talking to him about the case he let slip a bitter hatred of homosexuals. I immediately saw before me a likely reason why Hawkes had reacted as he did; hatred had been bred into him.

It can be seen from this case that all evidence, including expert and forensic, has to be treated with objectivity. It is by checking and cross checking and using some good old-fashioned common sense that the truth will be arrived at. The detective should never assume anything, nor be seduced by experts, but always seek informed opinion and remain his/her own man or woman. In the end it is the SIO who carries the can, and if the investigation comes off the rails, then the buck must stop with that SIO. Fortuna was once again my companion, not forgetting the first-class team she had blessed me with.

CHAPTER 21

The Recurring Case of Russell Causley

I am afraid that the saga of Russell Causley is not yet over. In February 1999, I was in my office at police headquarters, feeling pretty good with myself. I had somehow made it to the rank of detective superintendent; I was on call to deal with the next cold start murder to occur; chief constables' commendations bedecked my walls; everything was going so well. Then the phone rang. It was one of those phone calls a policeman doesn't want to receive. It was from the Criminal Cases Review Commission, an organisation which had been established in the mid-1980s to investigate allegations of miscarriages of justice which became prevalent during that decade. I was asked by the caller if I was involved in the case of Russell Causley, convicted of murder at Winchester Crown Court in December of 1996. With a lump in my throat I said, 'Yes.' I was told that a Mr Briggs had recently been questioned under oath in the witness box at a trial. He had been asked if he had ever at any time assisted the police, and he had replied, 'No.' In court at the time was a barrister who had also been in Winchester Crown Court in December 1996 when Mr Briggs had given evidence at the Causley trial. By Mr Briggs denying that he had ever assisted the police previously, doubt was raised about Causley's conviction, in that an important witness was effectively lying under oath. I was asked to preserve all material in the case including court exhibits and officers' note books. I couldn't believe it, after all that blood, sweat and tears, the whole job was going 'pear-shaped'. Worse was to come. The conspiracy theorists in the form of human rights lawyers, started asking questions about the other two (prisoner) witnesses. Because Mr Lomond wasn't prosecuted for the fraud he committed in Dorchester, whilst on the run from prison, it was assumed I may have deliberately let him off the hook. That decision not to prosecute him which I had religiously avoided not to get involved in had indeed come back to haunt me. Furthermore, Mr Briggs had received a discount on his sentence from the trial judge despite the fact that I had given sworn evidence at Winchester Crown Court that he had not. As I was the senior investigating officer, the buck stopped with me. It was also discovered that, unknown to me or my team, Murphy had also previously helped the police, despite denying this during the trial. About a week or so later I was served with a notice under the police discipline regulations setting out criminal allegations of perverting the course of justice, a crime for which if found guilty I would have been looking at five years' imprisonment at the minimum. I was not suspended from duty and was told the allegations were to be investigated by a team of CID officers from an outside force led by a detective superintendent.

The investigation team from the Wiltshire Constabulary did a mighty fine job. They seized every exhibit; re-interviewed witnesses and went through my pocket books and diaries, as well as those of my colleagues, with a fine-tooth comb. They found and uncovered nothing, absolutely nothing. No promises of reward for giving evidence, no dodgy deals to avoid prosecution, and the trump card of me misleading the trial judge at Winchester fell flat on its face. The judge in the trial of Mr Briggs had received a letter about his cooperation with the police in a murder case, but the letter was from the Crown Prosecution Service; I had never seen it, nor did I know such a letter existed. No text from me to the judge was ever found, simply because I didn't send one. I was interviewed by a detective chief superintendent and a detective sergeant for two and a half hours on tape and under caution for perverting the course of justice. The detective sergeant, a woman, gave me a particularly hard time; I thought her soul had been surgically removed. I answered every question put to me and declined the use of a solicitor. My good friend John Homer – of Taylor fame – the Superintendents' Association representative, thought I was mad and should have been legally represented, but I told him it would have taken me a week just to brief a solicitor and I hadn't done anything wrong anyway, so why did I need one?

Russell Causley's conviction was eventually set aside by the Appeal Court and a retrial ordered and he was given bail. My wife had lived with this nightmare of a job for years and I couldn't bring myself to tell her about all these recent developments, nor that I was subject to a pretty serious investigation. Then one evening she was watching the local television news which showed Russell Causley walking away from Winchester crown court having been admitted to bail, after attending an interim hearing. She said, 'That's Causley isn't it? What's he doing out?' I then had to tell her that there was some doubt about his conviction and I was being investigated for perverting the course of justice. She went white and nearly fell off the sofa. I spent the whole of that evening trying to convince her that I was not going to be sent to prison anytime soon!

While another force was investigating me, the Dorset Police set about reinvestigating the case of Causley and preparing for a new trial. This was led by Detective Superintendent Pete Jackson, (a former Para) who was ably assisted by Detective Sergeant Rawles, who, like Chris Stone, was one of the best in the force. The newly appointed prosecution barrister decided that the evidence from the three prisoners was too problematic and the new prosecution should proceed without them.

While all this was going on and just to pile on the grief, I was removed from CID to a small department called 'Community Safety'. This comprised a dedicated bunch of people who worked on crime prevention, and various community projects such as setting up 'youth shelters' in parks to give youngsters something to do. A big project they were undertaking involved a warehouse on an industrial estate, which contained all sorts of displays aimed at educating children of the dangers of crossing the road and not climbing down into road works and the like. The chief constable thought I would like my own department (of twelve people!) Call me old fashioned, but when I learned that my place on CID was to be taken by a 'Bramshill Flyer', that is a young in-service superintendent who had never been in the CID in his life but needed to show such experience on his CV before being promoted to assistant chief constable, I became a little cynical. The fact that this person was returning to the force from a secondment to Her Majesty's Inspector of Constabulary, who have great influence on chief constables, would of course have had nothing to do with it! It was clear that I had become toxic and once again remembered that success has many fathers but failure is an orphan. I realised that I had become not only yesterday's man, but the day before yesterday's man!

Before I went completely mad, an urge I had had years before came to fruition. In early 2000 I had seen an advertisement in Dorset Police General Orders inviting applications from superintendents to lead the British Forensic Team in Kosovo to assist with mass grave exhumations. The NATO invasion of Kosovo had taken place nine months earlier, and was, it must be said, a brave decision by Tony Blair who had in effect led the International Community to rescue the mainly Moslem Albanian population from genocide. As usual and typical of the story of my life, I didn't get the job. However, in July that year I was in the gym, (I had consigned beer and curry as the main off duty exercise of a CID man to the bin years before) when I saw Ian Coombes from the Personnel Department.

'Oh, hello, Tony,' he said, 'the Home Office phoned today to ask if you could take over the British Forensic Team in Kosovo for a couple of months, but I told them you were on leave in August.'

I nearly fainted. I couldn't believe the opportunity to be involved in such an important and world-shattering event had slipped through my fingers.

'Ian, forget my leave, forget everything. I want that job; phone them back now, please.'

I was reduced to begging. He abandoned his lunch break and made the call. Then when he did make the call the guy dealing with it in the Home Office was at lunch, so it was another agonising wait, but, yes, I got the job. Now all I had to do was wheedle round my deputy chief constable, George Pothecary to let me go. I think he knew I had drawn the shortest of short straws and was willing to release me for a couple of months.

In March 2004 Russell Causley once again stood trial for the murder of his wife. The defence argued for four days before a jury was sworn in, that he should not have to face a second trial. It was also alleged that he was suffering from signs of post-traumatic stress disorder and depression. The trial judge did not accept the arguments presented and ordered that the trial proceed. No evidence was heard in relation to Causley's conversations with the three convicted prisoners during his time in prison. However, one important witness did give evidence, that being his sister. Russell's father had died since the previous trial and there was no impediment to her telling the court about the vital words that she had heard her brother use 'I've killed one wife; I could kill another.' The jury returned a unanimous verdict of guilty to murder and before sentencing him for a second time, the trial judge, Her Honour Justice Hallett said the following: -

'What you did to your wife is beyond the understanding of most normal people. You bullied her and dominated her for years. You moved your mistress into the family home then involved your very vulnerable daughter in your sordid affair. The damage you have done to your daughter is incalculable, it's a miracle she has turned out as well adjusted as she has. Not only did you kill your wife and dispose of her body, you have left your daughter in a permanent state of ignorance as to her fate. You don't care about her feelings. The only feelings you care about are yours and Patricia Causley. When your daughter became too much trouble to you, she had to leave home. It's fortunate for her it wasn't worth your financial gain to kill her. In my mind you are a self-centred and calculating killer. You will do whatever you have to do to make your life easier. Your mistress appears to be of the same kind and I'm not surprised she hasn't dared to show her face at this court. In my judgement you are a wicked pair. This is cold blooded killing for financial gain.'

Justice Hallett then told Causley, 'It will be a minimum of 16 years before anybody should even consider your release. I'm not suggesting you'll ever be fit for release.' She also asked Prosecution Council to expedite the complaints against myself as they were clearly groundless.

Post Script

Following my good fortune to lead the British Forensic Team in Kosovo for seven weeks, I retired from the Dorset Police in 2001. I went on to work in various deployments in the Balkans and Middle East until 1999. My service and experience in the Met and Dorset prepared me for sights and experiences in these missions which were both upsetting and uplifting, all of which I will never forget; but that's another story.

On a cold, dull, grey day in early December 2014 I, was typing away at this book wearing an old cardigan, and a pair of soft baggy trousers with a hole in one knee when my front door was knocked in a firm manner. I wasn't expecting any one and was certainly not dressed to receive visitors. I answered the door to a well-dressed young man in a sharp crisp suit and silk tie; he introduced himself as Detective Sergeant Trevor Hawkins of the Dorset Police. Over the next three quarters of an hour he related to me the latest developments in a case I was all too familiar with. Russell Causley had recently received a phone call in prison from Patricia to say that she was aware he was being considered for parole, but if he was released, she would not be having him back. She was adamant that the relationship was over. Shortly after this news he appeared before the parole board who asked him why he should be considered for release as he had shown no remorse, nor disclosed the whereabouts of his wife's body. There and then he blurted out that he had strangled his wife after a furious row and burned her body in the back garden of their house in Ipswich Road, Bournemouth. He said the fire burnt for three days after-which he collected the ashes up and disposed of them around a local golf course. He mentioned that he had kept her body for a few days in an inspection pit in his garage before burning the corpse; this was the inspection pit that we had dug up, but ten years too late. The Dorset Police then re-opened an investigation into this case and any other people who may have been involved.

Russell Causley and his girlfriend Patricia were then interviewed by the police, but he stated that only one person was involved in the murder. What he did not do was to explain what he meant and would not clarify this point. The officers were not convinced by his explanations and as they got up to go, he winked at them. He was trying his games of power and control again and as will be seen shortly, laughing inside to himself at the officers.

Unbeknown to the police, Russell Causley had written to Patricia at the end of August 2014, after the parole board hearing and passionately expressed how hurt he was and how he longed to hear her voice. He still held out hope that she would come back to him. A month after the Dorset Police had visited him in December 2014, he wrote a detailed statement from his prison cell in Cambridgeshire. I have reproduced this statement verbatim below. However, although it was dated 23 January 2015, he did not release it immediately because he had set a trap for Patricia – he had sent her a letter requesting some small items of help. The last paragraph of the confession clearly displays that if there is a glimmer of hope he would let sleeping dogs lie and stay quiet. However, there was no response to his plea, so he released this statement to the authorities and thereby put on record that he blamed Patricia for killing his wife.

Russell Causley (A7852AC)
HMP Littlehey,
Perry,
Huntingdon,
Cambridgeshire
PE28 0SR
Friday 23rd January 2015
Statement History

I first met Tricia Causley (as she was then) back sometime in 1983. I was then attempting to start up a small insurance based company in Bournemouth along with a chap I had first met up with in London – Lee Green. Lee wanted to expand the work force and had advertised in the Bournemouth Echo which brought two responses, Trish being one. I had not wanted to expand the number of people working for us being extremely wary of the "claw back" system that existed in this type of business so I had said that Lee could do as he wished but that all profit and loss was his alone – he agreed. On the day of interviewing however; Lee asked me to take Tricia across the road from our office for a coffee while he interviewed the first young woman. After some half hour Lee collected Trish and that was that – I had found her chatty and quite personable, but nothing more than that. As it happened, I was put on baby-sitting duty with Trish once more a few days later when Lee called to say that he would be late for her second interview – I met her in the Round House bar again and again spent some half an hour or so with her – I left when Lee arrived. The third time that I spent with her was after she had joined the company and I ended up with her at her little flat after having dinner with her. We sat talking for maybe two hours or more – nothing else occurring – just talking – but on leaving I found that my brand-new car had somehow slipped its hand brake and rolled down the sloping road outside her flat until being stopped by a brick wall. The damage was not great but I was furious with myself – what was I doing spending half the night with this girl, a girl that I did not find that attractive. Tricia had followed me down to inspect the damage and said "I am so sorry, Russell – do you want a hug"? I replied "Yes I bloody well do." As I drove away I found that far from not finding her attractive I had fallen in love with this vibrant and personable red head. We started a full affair within days – first sleeping together on December 11th staying at the Hotel Cecil in Bournemouth.

I had returned from living in Canada in 1982 and had purchased a house in Suffolk which had proved to be a huge mistake hence the reason that I was living in a hotel in Bournemouth where we had previously lived before emigrating to Canada. I was actively looking for a new house so that we could all move back in 1983 – Tricia had seen the house I decided on even before my wife. I had asked my wife for a divorce even before meeting Trish as I had been having an affair with another woman for months but I was not in love with this lady and stopped seeing her the moment I met Tricia. Things at home were not good – Samantha and her mother were at each other's throats constantly, they hated each other with a vengeance and the fights both verbal and physical were a weekly, even daily feature of our lives. I made a dreadful mistake at this time – one that haunts me to this day – I introduced Samantha to Tricia and asked her to "keep my secret." The same day in the evening my wife came to me in tears and told me what had happened earlier – Samantha had come to her and said "Mummy if you have been told to keep a secret but you know its wrong, should you still keep it"? My wife imitated Samantha's whiney voice to perfection – she could not want to taunt her mother with this so hurtful information – I felt dreadful – I still do – along with the crime it is in my head always. Samantha used this information again and again, on one occasion screaming at her mother "You cannot even keep your fucking husband." I tried time and time again to get her to stop this but it was no use. – I had given her the ammunition to hurt her mother and she was going to keep on using it.

End of page 1 signed Russell Causley 23/01/2015

It was in this poisonous atmosphere that we entered 1985.

Tricia and I had been having our affair for some eighteen months and things could not go on for ever like that despite the fact that Carole *(Veronica Mary Packman)* and Tricia, paradoxically, got along very well given the circumstances. They had lived and worked together up in Yorkshire where we had done a three or four-month contract (the insurance business had folded and I had gone back into my old business of contract engineering) and often went out shopping together and so on. It has been said many times in court that I moved my "lover" into the family house, true and not true. When the insurance business had folded, we were months behind with our mortgage payments and in peril of losing the house. Tricia offered to sell her little flat and give "us" the money so as to stave off this happening. Tricia had to live somewhere and seeing as we were often not in the house and Tricia was able to baby sit Samantha while my wife and I worked away it was simply a solution, a quick fix.

I think that Carole was killed on a Sunday afternoon – I am not at all sure what month, but it was summer and that day and the days that followed were all warm and dry. The subject of solving the problem of our getting to live together by taking Carole's life and *(comment probably 'had')* been fully discussed many times and over several weeks. I had been stalling and vacillating while trying to find or come up with another way out of our situation. Tricia had become more and more frustrated over the months and no one who knows her can ever say that patience is her strong suit – she is very much a red head in character. On the day we had had yet another row or irritated talk and Tricia had given me an ultimatum? (my spell check has thrown this spelling out *(ultimation)* and I am too tired to work out why!) Either I do what had been discussed or I must go back to my wife. Her exact words were "I am going out for a short drive, either get it done or go back to your wife." I can hear those words and the tone used as clearly now as I did then. Tricia went out and I went up the stairs still not knowing or believing that I would do this awful thing. Carole was coming out of the small bedroom that we used as an office – something was said by her about Samantha or Tricia and I hit her knocking her out – I had never hit her before – ever. I then used a tie to cut off her airways there was not a sound from her – nothing.

I went down to the kitchen, I was in shock and shaking – Tricia arrived back – she had been gone for only a few minutes- fifteen to twenty no more. I said that I had done it and she went up-stairs to check and came down a few minutes later and I asked "Is she dead?" Tricia replied "She is now." There is no mistake in what she said and I took that to be an admission that she had acted to make sure having found a pulse or something. Trish had worked as some sort of nurse so I knew that she would know how to check – this remark was never brought up or mentioned again but the tie that I had used and which I had left lose was back around

Carole's neck and knotted when we went back up so I knew that there had to be signs of life when Tricia had checked. Did I care? No – lets be brutally honest- I did not, what did it matter? I had done all and everything to murder my wife and that's the truth of it. I have always known that this was in all probability an act undertaken by two people and not one. Today, all these years later it is only my word – the work *(comment probably word)* against Tricia's it is a moot point and totally unprovable but I have always known from day one and every year since that there was an argument for me to make against the charge of murder if I had chosen to disclose everything.

Tricia said that we had to move the body before Samantha arrived back home and so we went up and wrapped it up in two blankets taken from the airing cupboard in the small bedroom. Tricia folded Carole's legs back on themselves so as to make the final bundle smaller and less body-like. We then carried the body out of the house in broad daylight down the steps and placed it in the garage which we then locked.

A few minutes later we were sitting outside in the back garden. Tricia had brought a drink out for us both – wine or more probably gin and tonics – I sat there in the sunshine thinking that nothing seemed to have changed but of course everything had changed – it was an illusion.

I have been challenged on how I moved the body from the house. I do not know why seeing that Carole only weighed just over a hundred pounds. There were two of us doing the carrying. In

End of page 2 signed Russell Causley dated 230115

for instance – from the house to the garage but only myself the next day. Tricia having folded the legs back had thus reduced the length of the body and it was wrapped tightly. My wife was only five feet three inches tall and very slim – this is neither a heavy load to move nor large – its ghastly to write but if you are challenging me on this then you have to consider the size and weight – it was not difficult and I was very strong back in 1985.

The day after the murder I sat alone in the house with a problem – that is how I thought of it. Tricia had gone to work and left me with it. I sat in the kitchen and tried to come up with a solution – first idea – discussed with Tricia was to drive the body far, far away. But all too often one reads about dog walkers or ramblers stumbling across dead bodies. The solution came to me as I sat looking out of the window – I had piles of pine logs and very often had fires – I would burn the body. I have been challenged on this by Dorset Police and Mr English here in Littlehey, but regardless of the opinion of their scientist I can but repeat that (1) There was no smell or a large amount of smoke – nothing. (2) There was – after three days of keeping the fire going – no obvious residue – nothing. It took a week for the ash to go completely cold. I then took every last scrap of ash away in buckets and threw it all over the place, sometimes many miles from home. I do not care what the 'experts' say or think- I know what I saw and I know what was left – if there were small fragments of bone left – well I was obviously not looking for such, but I can but assure anyone reading this that there was nothing noticeable and most definitely no smell or extreme amounts of smoke, it was all too simple – I was staggered.

On her arrival home from work that evening I met Tricia in the drive outside the garage. After she got out of her car. I walked her to my own vehicle and went to open the boot. It was obvious to her that the body had been moved seeing as the garage was now open, but as I went to open the boot of my car Tricia said "Is this something that I really want to see?" I remember her words exactly – I simply opened the boot and showed it to be empty. Tricia asked "Where?" and I simply pointed to the fire up on the bank – it was in full blaze as it had been for hours. I cannot recall another word that may have passed between us – but those written above are exact – I have never forgotten them just as I have never forgotten her words when she put a gun to my head about "getting it done." There were very many conversations between us in the coming days. Tricia was fully involved and aware of all and everything that I did, especially my respect for forensic science – when the ash was cold, I removed all of it.

We then planned on how to make it look as if Veronica had simply had enough and left the house. Tricia was working up in London and I suggested that Samantha and I go up for a sightseeing trip and on all three of us returning "find" that Veronica had gone. The night before Tricia and I ripped up one special dress and started packing up many of my wife's clothes, shoes etc. In the morning all I had to do was turn back into the house on the pretext of having forgotten something and pull down the loft ladder (suitcases already moved out and hidden) and threw the prepared clothes around the bedroom, it all took less than two minutes. Samantha, like most teenagers, was still half asleep in the car and anyway Tricia was there to distract her if she tried to go back into the house. It all went as planned and we spent the day in London and picked up Tricia from her place of work after five and drove home. On finding the state of the house Samantha ran around like a banshee screaming out "She's gone, she's gone she's gone" she could not have been happier. I had left a letter written by Tricia purporting to be from Veronica along with her wedding ring on the kitchen work top – it all worked. Tricia had removed the wedding ring from her finger – not me – later saying that a spurned wife would most likely do that and that it would add authenticity to the note. This to me is a female's idea not a male – it's not something I would have thought of.

The idea that I could have acted alone is ridiculous, seeing as the risk of exposure on that morning of not one but two people suddenly deciding to run back up the steps and into the house on some pretext was extreme. How could I explain my actions? It would have all unravelled and I would have been arrested. It would only be feasible if one of the two people waiting in the car was fully alert and aware of the danger and able to stop Samantha, the only innocent party from moving from the car at the most critical time.

In the days between Christmas and New Year 1985 I called Bournemouth police to see if any

End of page 3 signed Russell Causley dated 230115

Information had come up regarding my wife's disappearance. I had reported her missing back in the summer and had been seen by the police sometime during the autumn, but had heard nothing from them. I was put through to an Inspector Vincent and he confirmed that Veronica had been in contact and was alive and well but did not want anything to do with me due to my affair with another woman. To say that I was amazed is to say the least – I was stunned – I now had proof from the best possible source that my wife had simply left me. Inspector Vincent later confirmed this conversation over the telephone to my then solicitor Anthony Hackett-Jones – I was home free or rather we were both home free.

Some people will likely dispute the cold-hearted wording I have put into Tricia's mouth – Tricia herself obviously – but on 17th July 2014 on a visit here at Littlehey and out of the blue said "I cannot do this anymore (visiting) I do not love you – I have met someone else (several years back in fact). He likes me and I like him (her exact wording). "I do not in fact even have any affection for you any-more." This was all delivered dry eyed and cold – very cold. I sat stunned – unable to even eat – I simply could not believe what I was being told – not one word had she ever said to me other than encouragement and love prior to this visit. *It* transpired that Samantha had put her name in the newspapers again and Tricia had panicked due to not wanting to lose her ability to work – she said "I will never be able to work again due to your daughter – I have had enough (and then this) "After all I did not do this."

Really? Well it's a fact is it not? I am the one who is sitting in jail convicted of murder and I am also the one that admitted that fact on August 1st 2015 *(comment 2014 he is confused on dates)*. Why would I do that if it was not entirely true? Well it's simply that I could not bear the thought of Tricia being blamed in any way – I have lived this lie for twenty years – carried the guilt for us both and frankly willingly so – I loved her that much – and what point was there in pointing the finger of blame at her now anyway? When Mr English came onto the wing to inform me that Tricia had been seen by Dorset Police back in December 2014 and had been informed, they intended to take no further action against her I said "Lucky girl" and laughed. Ask him. When Dorset Police had seen me sometime last year and asked their final question "Was anyone else involved in the murder?" I replied "No." But I was laughing again inside as the answer was true – it still is – there was only one person involved in the killing regardless of anything that might or might not have taken place after I left my wife's body lying on the floor of the upstairs landing. After my total break down at my parole hearing I did inform two inmates that I in fact did not do the actual murder. One did not pick up on it (I was in tears) the other did and he then went around telling other inmates and I had to scotch that very quickly – I still wanted to protect Tricia and thought that she would contact me in the days ahead of my parole hearing.

So "After all I did not do this "is very easily defended and frankly I do not care anymore and have not done so for years but let's get this straight. Who checked if Carole was in fact dead and made very sure? Who wrapped the body in blankets after making that check? Who was on the other end of the body bag which was carried out of the house in broad day light and placed it in the garage. Who impersonated Carole in front of a solicitor wearing a cheap blonde wig with no fear of being caught out by the real Carole turning up. When Tricia made this statement in the visits hall here in Littlehey I said "You must be delusional if you think that any court would accept *(spelt except)* that you were not fully involved if the facts were known even without the "Who did what "– only this week a young lad has got nineteen years for merely being in the street when his mate stabbed another lad." She sat there alert but then said "All my friends say that although they like you, I have done enough, stood by you long enough for all these years." I replied "And what would those same friends say if they knew the truth – that I have sat in prison protecting you, not doing course work and working with probation." Tricia replied "I don't think that they would talk to me anymore." I sat crying in the visits room and begged and begged her not to do this to me, all I wanted was those short telephone chats each week – an occasional visit and the extra money sent to help my existence. I would have stayed silent and died in jail quite happily. But my words and pleas are wasted. I was now the inconvenience to be removed it was 1985 revisited only I was the inconvenience that had to be removed. I loved this girl totally – still do and will for ever. I went back to me cell stunned and on the 19th July at around 3 am in the morning I wrote a six-page letter very similar to this one (since destroyed) – but far more emotional and the truth of what actually happened still shielded – I simply wrote that I had struck

End of page 4 signed Russell Causley dated 230115

the blow with my fist and then strangled my wife. I broke down at my parole hearing on August 1st and confessed to this terrible crime and said the same – I was still in bits – I had waited and waited for something from Tricia – I had hugged her and begged her to write to me saying that she would not abandon me totally – nothing. I did in fact hear from her weeks later – I had written explaining that what had broken me was not the "I do not love you" nor the "I have met someone else – he likes me and I like him" but the "I do not even have any affection for you anymore" in her reply she said that she did not mean that – really?

I did not know what to do, I just drifted along – when Dorset Police came calling, I still replied "No" when asked "Was anyone else involved?" So why the change? I cannot really say, I do not know – it's not revenge – although the "After all I did not do this" would perhaps bring that about. It has more to do with the promises that passed between us after I was arrested and then convicted. Tricia was very worried that I would tell the truth. I promised that I never ever would and she promised to stand by me likewise "for ever." Well a deal is a deal and I kept my part she broke her end of the bargain. I had carried this on my own for years and worked in the first few years assisting Tricia over the telephone to get back on her feet and earn the sort of living that we had enjoyed together rather than to work on my situation. I cared not at all for my problems – all I cared about, even worked on was addressing her on all and everything spending hours on the telephone to that end. I came up with the single most inventive brain wave I have ever had while on remand in Winchester – I knowing that Tricia was bi-sexual suggested that she go down to Brighton and endeavour to join that fraternity seeing as gay women look after their own. Trish bravely did just that and it worked. She got good contacts and better work – she coincidentally was eventually hired by a gay female at a bank, but that was as I have written only by coincidence. But regardless of that I advised her on all matters regarding work along with flats to move to – cars to purchase – house to find and then buy and so on. Trish has a very selective memory. This was frighteningly demonstrated several years ago. On my release back in 2002 we made a trip over to the Isle of Wight on a hundred-thousand-pound power boat owned by our then doctor in Maidenhead. Tricia actually took the controls on the way back from the island. I mentioned this trip to her some time back and she had not the slightest memory of it – nothing – so maybe in her mind she really did not do this.

I very rarely read anything to do with my crime – that way I do not have to face it, but prior to my parole hearing I did glance through several pages of old information and found myself amazed that no charge had ever been made against Tricia. There in print was Patricia Causley went into a solicitors' and pretended to be Carole Packman if that was known along with forging my wife's name on other documents why was no action ever taken – the strongest suspicion is there that Tricia had to know that my wife was not about to challenge her actions.

I fully understood just how much real affection Tricia had for me after I had been convicted and after some years had passed. I was incarcerated in HMP Gartree for four years and although Tricia either drove or trained past the prison on her way to Leeds each week I did not ask her to visit due to the rules making it a day away from her work. I did not wish to inconvenience her. In all those years she never once offered to come and see me – never once said "You must be lonely" or "I do not care about the inconvenience or lost money I want to see you." Not even at Christmas – nothing. I even had to constantly ask for an occasional card to be sent – anything to break my day – something – but even that was a struggle to her. I made those attempts on my life and still got nothing from her – no "Please don't do it." So, I have known for years how things were but I loved her so much that I chose to ignore the obvious and if not for her cold words last July would have gone on and on protecting her.

In this last week of January, I have written to Tricia asking for some help. I did so deliberately and to see what she would do. – It's now February 2nd and so far, I have heard nothing. – we shall see – her reaction will tell a story. It will also make my own mind up.

I have offered to 'tell all' to Dorset Police but I am wavering and when Mr English came to see me last week 30th of January I having misread what I had been given to read was quite

End of page 5 signed Russell Causley 300115

Ready to let sleeping dogs lie. I was in fact unhappy to realise that my offer was in fact being considered so I have written for some small items of help. If I get a reply then sleeping dogs can remain just that – this written statement will never be seen. If I hear nothing – as I fully expect – then seeing as Tricia has chosen to 'look after number one' why should I not choose to do the same? I might add that in choosing this that Tricia has looked after her own skin – in 1985 she wanted the life that I could offer and went for it – now I am simply an inconvenience one that is handicapping her ability to enjoy her life now.

Page 6 signed Russell Causley 5/2/2015

After these disclosures to the parole board, a four-part television mini-series *The Investigator: A British Crime Story* was screened by ITV in July 2016. This was a re-examination of the case and an attempt to answer the mystery of the whereabouts of his wife's body.

Considerable attention was focussed on some unsavoury sexual predilections of Russell Causley's which had no bearing on the murder of his wife. After the screening of this mini-series he withdrew his admissions, claiming that he was playing with the presenter. The Dorset Police did not accept the verbal and written statements made by Causley to the parole board, including his description of how he disposed of his wife's body, which they sought to counter with a forensic expert. A file of evidence was submitted by the Dorset Police to the CPS, who in December 2017 decided that it was not in the public interest to prosecute Patricia Causley (who now goes by another name, which I have chosen not to reveal) in relation to the forgery of the title deed documents on the house in Ipswich Road or any other offences.

I would like to finally turn to that confession of 23 January 2015 and examine it in a little more detail. This statement was only made after his relationship with Patricia had broken down; he had given her time to recant and when she did not, he made the written statement public. His motive was not to clear his conscience or set his daughter's mind to rest; it was one of spite. Statements made with such motivation and venom are looked upon with great suspicion by the courts and juries warned of the danger of convicting on such testimony. This statement must therefore be treated with extreme caution.

I have taken hundreds, perhaps thousands of confession statements both verbally and in writing from criminals over the years. What you are sure to get is a confession in which the criminal did not mean to cause the injury he did; he thought the girl wanted sex; he only did it because someone else led him astray; his mother didn't love him, he was damaged, he was unemployed; it goes on and on. But, in amongst that litany of excuses will be found the truth; that I believe to be the same in this case.

He described his wife's killing to have taken place in the summer of 1985. We discovered in the first investigation that the incident involving Samantha being taken to London and Veronica's torn red dress being found with her wedding ring on their return to Bournemouth from this day trip, took place on or about 15 June 1985. We know she was last seen alive by her solicitor of Ward Bowie when she raised the issue of a divorce on 14 June 1985; so, Russell Causley's recall of the time when the murder happened is exactly when we deduced it to have happened. It should be remembered that at this time he was experiencing acute financial problems as well as the strain caused by the break-down of the marriage. The notice of impending divorce would have brought with it the realisation that that he would also lose half the equity in the marital home.

On the day of the murder he described how Patricia nagged him to get rid of Carole and gave him an ultimatum to get it done or she would leave him. He stated that her exact words were 'I am going out for a short drive, either get it done or go back to your wife.' He then recounted going up the stairs and having a row with his wife; he blamed Sam again as the cause. Without further explanation he says he gave her a punch to the head which rendered her unconscious and then strangled her with a tie until there was no sound from her. He made it sound like an almost painless procedure. It is interesting to remember that he told the convicted prisoner Murphy, that he gave his wife a whiff of gas before putting a bag over her head and asphyxiating her. In both cases the victim was unconscious before oxygen was denied to the lungs. In my view and in common with many confessions I have taken, he is minimising what he has done, or trying to make it sound as painless as possible. Whether he struck a blow I do not know, but that he strangled her is highly likely. Whilst he denied ever having hit his wife, we uncovered disclosures made by Veronica to friends and others that she was the victim of domestic violence, as was Samantha. Evidence was offered to the court in 1996 but was considered to be hearsay and excluded from the jury.

He next related the return of Patricia to the house and him telling her that he had done it! He stated that she went upstairs and when she came back down, he asked, 'Is she dead?' to which she replied, 'She is now.' He then said that he went back upstairs and found the tie around his wife's neck was knotted and not loose as he said he had left it. The clear implication is that his wife was still alive when he came down stairs and had in fact been strangled by Patricia. So, he had not killed her at all; Patricia had. So, far from a confession and admission of guilt, he is saying that he has not murdered his wife. Patricia was the killer.

Moving next to the disposal of the body; he clearly implicated Patricia in moving the body and gives quite intimate detail how the victim's legs were folded back to facilitate the carrying of her to the garage. It is here the body was stored – out of the house – until burning on a fierce fire the next day. All this is very plausible, was admitted verbally in his spontaneous outburst to the parole board and the very fact that a fire burnt for several days was corroborated by Samantha. She clearly remembers this fire which also included ornamental bamboo, which she thought at the time should not have been cut down and she precisely knew the site of the fire. Causley clearly stated in his confession that he respects forensic science and removed all of the ash going into detail how this was done. It will be recalled once again that Murphy told the crown court at Winchester in 1996 that Causley was concerned about the police finding traces of his wife's DNA and had disposed of her body in acid. While the method was different, it was to the same purpose and with the growing knowledge of the police use of DNA at that time. I find the disposal of Veronica's body on a bonfire convincing. Humans have been disposing of corpses on funeral pyres from time immemorial and still do today, particularly in the Far East. This murder took place over thirty-eight years ago and the garden was heavily landscaped with earth moving machinery after he sold it. The unfortunate fact is that there is just nothing left to find.

Midway through his statement he shows clear delight in laughing at authority. He laughed inside when he was earlier told that the Dorset Police would be taking no action against Patricia. He found it amusing again, when he told the police that no one else was involved in the murder – secretly saying inside to himself that it was Patricia, not him. He ended the statement with this game playing when he described the trap he laid for Patricia, when asking for help with small items. He could not stop trying to manipulate people from his prison cell, just like he did when he fed the convicted fraudster Briggs with the cock and bull story about burying Veronica's body in the New Forest. His desire to exercise control over others is evident throughout his life; it is who he is. But, don't forget the lesson of the red squirrel; do not take your eye off it.

Russell Causley in his exhaustive statement of 23 January 2015 went into great detail about his own actions and that of Patricia in relation to the murder of his wife and that of the disposal of her body. He agonised for pages about how much he felt for Patricia and how deeply he was hurt by her rejection of him. He gives not one glimmer of any remorse for killing his beautiful wife, not one mention. Russell Causley, in my experience, exhibits the characteristics and lack of empathy of a psychopath, he is a games player who lost the game. He committed the perfect murder – almost!

Index